Sôhkêyihta
The Poetry of Sky Dancer Louise Bernice Halfe

Sôhkêyihta
The Poetry of Sky Dancer Louise Bernice Halfe

Selected
with an
introduction by
David Gaertner
and an
afterword by
Sky Dancer Louise Bernice Halfe

LAURIER POETRY SERIES

**WILFRID LAURIER
UNIVERSITY PRESS**

Wilfrid Laurier University Press acknowledges the support of the Canada Council for the Arts for its publishing program. We acknowledge the financial support of the Government of Canada through the Canada Book Fund for our publishing activities. This work was supported by the Research Support Fund.

Library and Archives Canada Cataloguing in Publication

Halfe, Louise Bernice, 1953–
[Poems. Selections]
    Sôhkêyihta : the poetry of Sky Dancer Louise Bernice Halfe / selected with an introduction by David Gaertner ; and an afterword by Sky Dancer Louise Bernice Halfe.

(Laurier poetry series)
Includes some words in Cree.
Issued in print and electronic formats.
ISBN 978-1-77112-349-5 (paperback).—ISBN 978-1-77112-351-8 (epub).—
ISBN 978-1-77112-350-1 (pdf)

    I. Gaertner, David, 1979–, editor II. Title. III. Series: Laurier poetry series

PS8565.A4335A6 2018   C811'.54   C2017-907833-X
                                             C2017-907834-8

Cover photo by Nelly Volkovich.
Cover design and text design by P.J. Woodland.

This book is printed on FSC® certified paper and is certified Ecologo. It contains post-consumer fibre, is processed chlorine free, and is manufactured using biogas energy.

Printed in Canada

Every reasonable effort has been made to acquire permission for copyright material used in this text, and to acknowledge all such indebtedness accurately. Any errors and omissions called to the publisher's attention will be corrected in future printings.

RECYCLED
Paper made from
recycled material
FSC® C103567

Table of Contents

Foreword

The Laurier Poetry Series was conceived in 2002 as a means to celebrate Canadian poetry and to introduce new readers to the richness and diversity of its poets. Rather than curate another large anthology that featured only a few poems by each poet, we thought it a good idea to suggest the real range of a poet's work by enlarging the selection. Our anthology would have to comprise many volumes. But why stick with a many-volumed anthology? Why not create a series of small and affordable "selected"s? Each volume could be introduced by a knowledgeable and reader- and poet-friendly critic in greater depth than in normal anthologies, and each could provide space for the poet to respond or participate in an additional way by contributing an afterword such as no standard anthology could offer.

Readers could pick and choose which poets they wanted to explore; instructors could also pick and choose combinations of volumes in a package for their students – and could change this selection from semester to semester. And the volumes could reach an international audience. Each would also have the potential to open out onto other books by the featured poet.

That was the blueprint. The Series was launched in 2004, with Catherine Hunter's selection of the poetry of Lorna Crozier, *Before the First Word*. There have been over twenty-five volumes since, offering introductions to a wide range of poets and poetries, and more are in the works. The Laurier Poetry Series is now the most comprehensive collection of Canadian poetries in print anywhere. Most volumes are also available as digital editions.

The consummate professionalism of the team at Wilfrid Laurier University Press, especially Managing Editor Rob Kohlmeier, has ensured that these sometimes technically tricky volumes are presented accurately and beautifully.

What continues to inspire us about the LPS is its reception across the country. The love and art and passion and intimacy that twenty-five-plus editors and twenty-five-plus poets have brought to their volumes; the innumerable hours and conversations and meetings, the thousands of emails between and among poets and editors and the staff at WLU Press; the generous reviews in the country's journals; the reception in classrooms and beyond: all of this eloquently speaks to the joyful proliferation of poetry in Canada today.

With each new volume, LPS hopes to continue to recognize the growing provenance of this wealth, the wide range of these riches. Our poets – and their readers – deserve nothing less.

—Brian Henderson and Neil Besner
General Editors

Biographical Note

Sky Dancer Louise Bernice Halfe is a Cree poet and social worker based just outside of Saskatoon. She was born in 1953 in Two Hills, Alberta, and was raised on the Saddle Lake Reserve on Treaty Six territory. At the age of seven she was taken from her home to attend Blue Quills Residential School (St. Paul, Alberta), where she remained for nine years. She began writing about her experiences in journals as a high school student, a practice that would eventually awaken her to a life as a poet: "I didn't choose poetry," Halfe tells Cree and European poet Selina Boan. "Poetry came nodding its head in when I was keeping a journal. The journal writing kept calling to me and was reinforced by dreams and ceremony."[1]

Halfe published her first poems in *Writing the Circle: Native Women of Western Canada* (NeWest Press), a collection of stories, poems, essays, and bibliographical pieces written by Indigenous women. This was followed by work published in *Residential Schools: The Stolen Years* (University of Saskatchewan, News & Publications Office), a collection of writing by residential school survivors, including Janice Acoose, Phil Fontaine, and Maria Campbell. Her first book, *Bear Bones & Feathers*, was published by Coteau Books in 1994 and won the Canadian People's Poet Award and the Milton Acorn Award. Halfe has published four critically acclaimed books of poetry, including *Bear Bones, Blue Marrow* (1998/2004), *The Crooked Good* (2007), and *Burning in This Midnight Dream* (2016). *Blue Marrow*, originally published by McClelland & Stewart, was a finalist for the Governor General's Award and won the Pat Lowther Memorial Award. Halfe republished the book six years later with Coteau Books (where her work has primarily lived ever since), adding a Cree-to-English glossary and nine new pages of text. In 2005, she was chosen as Saskatchewan's Poet Laureate, only the second person ever to hold that post, and in 2012 she received an honorary Doctor of Letters (DLitt) from Wilfrid Laurier University. In 2016 she was a recipient of a Hnatyshyn Foundation REVEAL award, given in recognition of Indigenous artists living in Canada. In 2017 she was awarded the Latner Writer's Trust Award in recognition of a remarkable body of work. *Burning in This Midnight Dream* continues a long poetic engagement with residential schools and makes a significant intervention into the discourse surrounding the Truth and Reconciliation Commission of Canada (TRC): "[T]hese poems are testimonies of truth, justice and healing," former TRC senior researcher Paulette Regan writes. "They give us hope."[2]

Social work also plays an important role in Halfe's life and in her poems. She received her bachelor of Social Work from the University of Regina and has certificates in drug and alcohol counselling from the Nechi Institute: "I use my social work skills to help others and to enrich my writing career," she tells Boan. "They feed one another."[3] Halfe is currently the acting Elder at the University of Saskatchewan and travels widely across Canada and internationally. She lives with her husband and is the mother of two children and grandmother of three boys.

Notes

1   Selina Boan, "Louise Bernice Halfe," *Nineteen Questions*, https://nineteenquestions .com/2017/06/21/louise-bernice-halfe/
2   Paulette Regan, Foreword, *Burning in This Midnight Dream.*
3   Boan, ibid.

Introduction

"Listen to the bones"

— Sky Dancer Louise Bernice Halfe, *Blue Marrow*

Sky Dancer Louise Bernice Halfe breathes life into silence. For more than twenty-five years, Halfe, who is Cree, from the Saddle Lake Reserve and Treaty Six territory, has used Cree poetics to delicately craft voice out of silence: out of the unheard, out of the ongoing violence of Canada's colonial history, and out of the repression administered in Canadian residential schools. Halfe, like her narrators, "hung[ers] / for voice" in a system designed around famine; perhaps more than any other poet in Canada, Halfe captures the danger that Indigenous peoples risk in breaking colonial silence. But while it bears witness to the unsaid, Halfe's poetry also makes plain the labour, love, and healing that Indigenous people – particularly Indigenous women – dedicate to the sharing of language, stories, and history. The poems in this collection, while a small sample of the breadth of Halfe's work, aim to capture the poet's ongoing engagement with the unsayable while highlighting the intimate, healing spaces she carves out with her words.

Poetry traces out the unsayable. It outlines silence. It darts in and out between the perimeters of the impossible. But the unsayable that Halfe contends with is not always of the order derived from the Romantic tradition – although it does often reach toward the divine. Like residential schools, which are only a symptom of a larger, more systemic problem, the colonial narrative itself is always threatening to silence and erase Indigenous voices. Canadian poetry plays its own role here. Take, for instance,

Duncan Campbell Scott: on one hand, as the author of poems such as "The Onondaga Madonna," he is lauded as one of Canada's great "Confederation Poets." On the other hand, as the deputy superintendent of Indian Affairs, he is rightfully deplored as an architect of residential schools. Scott's poetics (and his politics; each is inseparable from the other) aimed at assimilating and effacing Indigenous presence: "I want to get rid of the Indian problem," Scott famously wrote.[1] Read within the larger context of Canadian poetry, it becomes evident that when Halfe writes of the ineffable, or the barely effable, she's not attesting to the failure of language to capture and represent a thing, she is writing, more specifically, of the difficulty of Indigenous self-determination within political and poetic systems of *terra nullius* that actively work to erase and repress it.[2] In this sense, finding voice, for Halfe, is not simply about speaking around and through settler colonialism, but, more paradoxically, about silence.

Residential schools were designed, quite literally, to silence Indigenous peoples via violent assimilation policies. Students were punished for speaking in the language of their communities; siblings were separated and forbidden to communicate; even letters home were read by staff and edited for content.[3] In his classic history of residential schools, *Shingwauk's Vision*, published in 1996, the historian J.R. Miller unearthed records documenting an Oblate principal's insistence that residential school students remain "in silence practically all the time."[4] Records also show that, as punishment for speaking her language, an Anishinaabe student was forced to write, "I won't talk Indian anymore" five hundred times, under the threat of "be[ing] strapped, or made to kneel in a corner for half an hour."[5]

How does one articulate this kind of silence? Words that have been stolen away or buried deep inside? Experiences that never can or never will be spoken? How does a poet trace out these lines? As the backdrop against which Indigenous voices are cast, the silence that historians have identified in Canada's residential school system is rendered even more frighteningly lucid in survivor testimony such as Halfe's and her contemporaries'. In *Residential Schools: The Stolen Years* (1993), a collection of writing by residential school survivors, including Halfe, Janice Acoose, and Maria Campbell, Acoose speaks to the silence that resonates out of those schools: "As a child, I tried to tell anyone who would listen about those night visits to our dorm, the cruel punishments, and the deadly threats, but my voice was silenced by my family's fears, the community pressure, and the church's power. As a result I grew up believing that what I felt, heard, and saw was not real."[6]

Acoose's testimony documents the ways in which silence permeates survivor consciousness, calling into question the possibility of their experiences, and upending their connections to the real. Halfe's early work contends with the residential school experience – and the pervasive silence that quickly became reality for many students – but always with an eye toward healing.

Like Acoose and her parents before her, Halfe is a residential school survivor. She was taken from her home at the age of seven to attend Blue Quills Residential School, a federally sponsored and church-operated school in St. Paul, Alberta. Her experiences at Blue Quills would go on to form the basis of much of her writing: from early poems such as "The Residential School Bus" (1993) and "Returning" (1993), first published in *Residential Schools,* to her 2016 collection, *Burning in This Midnight Dream* – which contends explicitly with survivor experiences in the context of the Truth and Reconciliation Commission.

In her first published work, released in *Writing the Circle: Native Women of Western Canada* (1990), silence takes shape as an interlocutor. The poem "Valentine Dialogue" is a dialogue in name only, given that there is only one speaker, an Indigenous woman suffering from sexual abuse. Emulating the confessional, a recurrent theme in these poems, the narrator speaks to an unseen, and, in this case, unheard recipient. "Valentine Dialogue" uses the rez-english that Halfe will go on to perfect in *Blue Marrow* in order to tell this story:

> Dired of dis crucifixion
> Dew ya dink confession will help?
> Dew ya dink penance will clean me?
> Maybe I'll be born again.
> Guild, guild.
> Da pain in my heart
> hurts hurts.

In focusing on Catholicism and the confessional, the narrator of "Valentine Dialogue" draws attention to the ways in which guilt and voice are linked under settler colonialism as a means to silence Indigenous women. In order to perceive herself as "clean," the narrator of this poem must articulate abuse committed against her as her own sin, rather than the depravity of the perpetrator. Speaking out therefore becomes a matter of speaking in, inasmuch as the means for bearing witness to abuse necessitates the narrator falsely implicating herself.

However, "Valentine Dialogue" is not simply a treatise on repressive colonial practices. It also demonstrates how Indigenous voices defy the silences of settler colonialism and generate spaces of resistance and love. For instance, "guilt" comes out as "guild" in the narrator's dialect. Heard as "guild," the second half of this passage cannot be read only as an admission of culpability, or remorse; it is also an appeal to a community to help her contend with the pain she is experiencing. In this sense, the reader is identified as the second half of the "dialogue" named in the poem's title. The potential for resistance and renewal thus comes down to a matter of community built within the structure of the poetics themselves: as a matter of hearing, engaging, and bearing witness.

In the even deeper solitude of their perspective, however, the poems in *Residential Schools* convey a very different sense of alienation and loneliness than "Valentine Dialogue." A detached observer-narrator, who provides a fly-on-the-wall point of view of the student experience in residential schools, relates "The Residential School Bus." In its sparse descriptions, short stanzas, and brusque line breaks, the poem brings form and content together to depict the profound estrangement experienced by students within the walls of residential schools:

> At night the little ones
> press their bodies
> between cold starched sheets.
> Somewhere
> someone
> in the huge dorm
> sobs quietly.

Punctuated by purposefully vague descriptors ("somewhere," "someone") sequestered in single lines of verse, "The Residential School Bus" proffers a cold, antiseptic space that strips children of their identity and connection to place: they become no one, nowhere. Indeed, while bodies and people take up a large portion of the space in this poem, silence is the primary character. The only mention of sound lies in these final lines, with "quiet sobs" and an earlier mention of an "echo" in a "long white empty hallway." The entire poem feels as if it is taking place in an oversized vacuum. The silence is dense, palpable, and smothering, but out of it Halfe traces the outlines of resurgence. Through the voices that lead us out of the darkness toward the possibility of healing hope is rooted in the truth of these experiences.

Indeed, Halfe's narrators, like Halfe herself, dedicate themselves to pushing silence back, (re)inserting themselves into the colonial narrative in order for Indigenous stories, Indigenous languages, and Indigenous peoples to survive, thrive, heal, and grow. But battling back against silence does not come without a cost. The emotional energy and risk required in undertaking the labour of voice is conveyed in a vignette from *Blue Marrow*, told by âcimowinis, Keeper of the Stories. In this excerpt, an Indigenous woman shares a story about attending, with her children, the family reunion of her white husband. Each member of her husband's extended family "has brought a book they've lovingly compiled," and as the settlers convene, they reread and, in doing so, re-substantiate the "heroics" of the colonial project:

> … Laughter and wonder
> as fingers move across the atlas. This is where
> great-granddad Arne crossed on the barge.
> This is where great-great-granddad travelled
> and preached the law of the land where his
> wife Isobel taught the little savages to read.

It is not a coincidence that each member of the white family carries a book in this passage. According to the Creek scholar and author Elizabeth Cook-Lynn, "the invasion of North America by European peoples has been portrayed in history and literature as a benign movement directed by God, a movement of moral courage and physical endurance, a victory for all humanity."[7] Of course, the (re)telling of this "benign" narrative, which Halfe captures in the above excerpt, is anything but. Told and retold, settler stories of courage and endurance naturalize and glorify systems that displace, dehumanize, erase, and silence Indigenous people – even when, as in Halfe's story, Indigenous people are in the room as these stories are told. In this sense, uncritical tellings of the colonial narrative re-enact colonialism in that they contribute to the erasure of Indigenous presence and the persistent ideologies of *terra nullius*.

So how do Halfe's poems breathe? According to Anishinaabe critic Niigaanwewidan James Sinclair, "Indigenous poetics are the intricate and intellectual acts of gifting words full of breath, rhythm and expression in the hopes they will be accepted in a world constituted by language."[8] To write against colonialism is to find oneself in a room in which the walls are perpetually closing in. Yet within Halfe's poems, we get a deep sense of breath, of rhythm, of love, and of restoration. In the reunion excerpt, for instance, quoted above, Halfe's Indigenous narrator and her children find themselves at the centre of a colonial storytelling project. The feeling of erasure is palpable for the narrator, as the stories from the settlers' books and maps quite literally white out Indigenous histories before her eyes. The poem concludes with âcimowinis attempting to remedy the imposed whiteout by weaving a healing counter-narrative for her children:

> I tell them
> how my relatives lived around the fort,
> starving and freezing,
> waiting for diluted spirits
> and handouts from my husband's family.
> I tell them
> how their little children died wrapped in
> smallpox blankets.
> My breath
> won't come anymore.
> I stare
> at the wheatfields.

Form and content come together as this section of *Blue Marrow* draws to a close. While the lines beginning the passage are long and descriptive, the majority of them containing ten to fifteen syllables, subsequent lines are much shorter, with fewer syllables, when âcimowinis begins to share her Indigenous histories. Those lines echo the loss of breath she describes in the penultimate sentence: "my breath / won't come anymore."

Indeed, breath and whitespace are intimately linked in this scene. Whitespace, the area of a page unoccupied by text or an image in a poem, is an important element of any poet's craft. However, for Indigenous poets, in the context of silence and *terra nullius*, it takes on political contexts and meanings: "this chosen walk is a blizzard whiteout. / My Cree-ing alone in the heavy arm of snow," Halfe writes in *Blue Marrow*, emphasizing the struggle of Indigenous poets to push back against settler narratives and to nurture Indigenous voices in a colonial landscape. The wheatfields, that great symbol of agricultural development and therefore of settler "ownership" of the land, are a literal example of whitespace as it marks the prairies. They physicalize the narrator's silence at the end of the reunion scene. Mirroring the colonial landscape, then, whitespace creeps into this poem as part of its structure and rhythm as well, punctuating the narratives that âcimowinis attempts to share and, at a gradually increasing rate, generating the effect of a story told between desperate gulps of air ("my breath / won't come anymore / I stare / at the wheatfields"). The reader can hear how the short lines are punctuated by the speaker's gasps. Yet the take-away from this excerpt is not the narrator's *loss* of breath – it is the very fact *of* her breath. That fact is the love with which she pushes back against silence and whitespace in order to share these stories, these âcimowinisa, with her children. As Sinclair puts it, the words in these poems are gifts of breath, passing from poet to reader through the lobes and alveoli of Halfe's poetics. As the breath moves – in and out, in and out – between Halfe, and text, and reader, these poems become acts of resuscitation and renewal.

In this sense, Halfe's commitment to breath and story also constitutes a poetics of witnessing. According to Kwagiulth (Kwakwaka'wakw) scholar and activist Sarah Hunt, bearing witness, in an Indigenous context, is a means of holding oneself accountable to one's community: first, by listening attentively to the stories and accounts of history that go unheard in the broader public discourse, and, second, by amplifying those voices and sheltering them against the din of settler colonialism. According to Hunt, "witnessing ... might be understood as a methodology in which we are obligated, through a set of relational responsibilities, to ensure frameworks of representation allow for the lives we have witnessed to be made visible."[9] In witnessing Indigenous stories, Hunt goes on to write, "[we are] obligated to ensure they are not denied, ignored or silenced."[10]

As a witness to colonial history and for Indigenous people (namely Indigenous women and children), Halfe's poetry is a conduit for silenced voices. Bearing witness, as it is defined across Halfe's works, therefore often means holding space for those who cannot speak, or, more radically, holding space for the dead: "Weep for those who haven't yet sung," Halfe writes in *Burning in This Midnight Dream*: "Weep for those who will never sing." In *Blue Marrow*, for instance, the narrator testifies to her position as medium for – or, more succinctly, *as* – a collector and inheritor of these voices:

My hunt is without a rifle,
without a net,
my bone
filled with the fists of women
of the fur trade.

The bone in this passage stands in for the pen through which Halfe
testifies to the experiences of Indigenous women, women who can no
longer speak for themselves, women who are dead and dying because
of the ongoing effects of colonialism. "Blue marrow" is the ink that fills
Halfe's pen. The stories she writes, or perhaps translates, are written with
the bones of the dead – their marrow her ink. In this sense, Halfe is also
writing, quite literally, with the "blue quills" of her residential school
experience – re-appropriating a tool of colonial silence to bear witness
to the attempted erasure of Indigenous children. Like the bones, or as an
extension of the bones, blue quills and blue marrow become instruments
through which to mark and hold up Indigenous experience.

As a methodology, or a "recipe for voice," as she identifies it in *Bear
Bones & Feathers*, Halfe's poetics of witnessing gives voice to those who
have been forced into silence, or who have lost their lives to the colonial
system. Significantly, then, Halfe also bears witness for the children of resi-
dential schools who will never have the opportunity to share their stories,
or for whom testimony to their experiences in those schools is impossible.
In *The Crooked Good*, for instance, she shares the story of *wiyipiyiniw*, or
"filthy man," a residential school survivor whose experiences were so trau-
matic that he cannot find the will or the words to express them:

> I was shipped to St. Judas. Spoke little English,
> hid my Cree. Cut my braids. I thought someone died.
> I wanted charcoal to paint my cheeks. Father-What-A-Waste
> became a hornet, unbuckled his belt. My breath ran those
> hallways. I fought. His neck was a cobra. Sister threw ice water, a
> scrub brush, lye soap. I burned. Forced cod-liver oil.
> I vomited and vomited. Licked the floor.
> Sacred old man buggered me. Bastards. How can I share this?

Wiyipiyiniw's story captures the atrocities of residential schools, the sexual
and physical abuse that ran rampant in these spaces,[11] and, more impor-
tantly, it marks their (im)possibility – by which I mean their actualization

in testimony. Indeed, the story ends with an open recognition of this voice, and voices like it, as ghostly presences in the narrative, marked by italics and set off from the rest of the poem. The narrator himself also acknowledges the impossibility of registering his story, even as he attempts to mark it: "How can I share this?" he questions. How does he, and how do we, now, as inheritors of this story, bear witness to the impossible?

In the poems in this collection, Halfe brushes us against the Truths that escape the capture of language. She calls us, as readers, to bear witness to the violence of residential schools and settler colonialism writ large. When she demands that we "listen to the bones," the quotation that opens this introduction and this collection, Halfe asks that we bear witness to those who cannot speak, and who will not speak. Importantly, the imperative is not a demand for others to make their voices heard. It is not a call for those who have been harmed to reopen their wounds by sharing their stories. It is a petition to hear and to listen, as Halfe herself does – closely and compassionately – to silence.

Notes

1 First Nations Child and Family Caring Society of Canada, n.p.
2 At the onset of colonialism, *terra nullius* (literally, no man's land) was a legal definition, a means of erasing Indigenous presence on a territory so that settlers could claim it. For Métis author and critic Warren Cariou, however, *terra nullius* is not simply a historical reference; it has deep resonance in contemporary settings as well, including literary spaces: "Indigenous space has become *terra nullius* in terms of being a wasteland, as something that doesn't even register in the colonial mindset at all," Cariou writes (35). *Terra nullius*, as it exists today, is the persistent and ongoing erasure of Indigenous presence from the land, from the history, from literature, and from language.
3 Miller, 311.
4 Miller, 202.
5 Miller, 204.
6 Acoose, 6.
7 Cook-Lynn, 29.
8 Sinclair, 208.
9 Hunt, 1.
10 Hunt, 9.
11 Truth and Reconciliation Commission of Canada, 103–12.

Works Cited

Acoose, Janice. "Deconstructing Five Generations of White Christian Colonial Rule." *Residential Schools: The Stolen Years*. Edited by Linda Jaine, University Extension Press, University of Saskatchewan 1993, pp. 3–13.

Cariou, Warren. "Edgework: Indigenous Poetics as Re-placement." *Indigenous Poetics in Canada*. Edited by Neal McLeod, Wilfrid Laurier UP, 2014, pp. 31–38.

Cook-Lynn, Elizabeth. "Why I Can't Read Wallace Stegner." *Why I Can't Read Wallace Stegner and Other Essays*, edited by Cook-Lynn, University of Wisconsin Press, 1996, pp. 29–40.

First Nations Child & Family Caring Society of Canada. "The Legacy of Duncan Campbell Scott: More Than Just a Canadian Poet." July 2016. fncaringsociety.com/sites/default/files/Duncan%20Campbell%20Scott%20Information%20Sheet_FINAL.pdf.

Hunt, Sarah. "Researching within Relations of Violence: Witnessing as methodology." *Contexts of Indigenous Research*. Edited by D. McGregor and R. Johnston, forthcoming.

Miller, J.R. *Shingwauk's Vision: A History of Native Residential Schools*. U of Toronto P, 1996.

Perreault, Jeanne, and Sylvia Vance. *Writing the Circle: Native Women of Western Canada*. NeWest Publishers, 1990.

Sinclair, Niigaanwewidan James. "The Power of Dirty Waters: Indigenous Poetics." *Indigenous Poetics in Canada*. Edited by Neal McLeod, Wilfrid Laurier UP, 2014, pp. 203–16.

Truth and Reconciliation Canada. *Honouring the Truth, Reconciling for the Future: Summary of the Final Report of the Truth and Reconciliation Commission of Canada*. Truth and Reconciliation Commission of Canada, 2015.

Crying for Voice

I must pull frog
pry its webbed feet
from snails in
my throat.

Kneel, fold my hands
invite weasel to untangle
my braids.

Boil duck, rabbit, fish
scoop out brain,
eyes and tongue
roll them
inside my gut.

Pull out tapeworm
chop onions, grind peppercorns
fill the intestine
with fresh blood.

Boil bible and tripe
clean off grass,
boil and boil
pebbles bubbling
soup.

Suck marrow from tiny bones
fill the place
where frog left slime
and salted snails
fell.

I'm fluttering wind
tobacco floating
against my face
mosquitoes up my nostrils
swatting memories
inside marrow.

The Residential School Bus

A yellow caterpillar,
it swallows them up.

The little brown ones their stained
faces in the windows   skinny and thick
black braids   pressing hands
grease the glass.

On its back the caterpillar
carries hand-sewn canvas bags.

Outside against the evening sun
the mothers, the fathers,
shrink.

They cannot look
at the
yellow caterpillar.

      * * *

The building is huge
with long white empty hallways.

A child walks softly
the echo runs ahead of her.

The smell of Lysol
and floor wax
overwhelms the memory of wood smoke
and dirt floors.

      * * *

At night the little ones
press their bodies
between cold starched sheets.
Somewhere
someone

in the huge dorm
sobs quietly.

The child
clenches
two purple
suckers
underneath her pillow.

She won't eat them,
not for a
while.

     * * *

They line up for breakfast
and receive wonderful bowls of porridge.

She loves porridge.
Her mama always made her porridge.

She looks up and sees
her favourite brother.

Ivan's ears look like
two gliding hawks.
They've given him a crew cut.

Charlie the eldest brother
is in the big boy's room.
She doesn't see him
and doesn't care.

Her eyes linger on
Ivan. They smile.

She swallows
the porridge
that is stuck in her
throat.

     * * *

Geesuz
is always mad.

She sits too often
in the confessional.
She kneels too often
in front of geesuz.

     * * *

The vision box
collects people
and makes them dance.

She turns the buttons
and the dancing people
turn into black and white lines.

She kneels
in the corner.

The girl
with the mean stick
and fat mouth
hovers near her.
She's a
huge night moth
beating her wings
against the dance.

     * * *

They've arrived.
Wagonloads of
mothers, of fathers.

The children have been
berry picking.

Sister Treebow
is like that girl
with the big lips.

Sister's lips stick out
further. The arrival of
mothers, of fathers
makes her madder.

The children
stand around the corner
of the building
wondering whose
mother, whose father
was there.

She didn't want to hope.

Father Brown
in his long black dress
calls out names.

Times are scheduled.

In the bare parlor
they sit,
mother, father, Ivan
and her big brother.

Their stiff hugs,
she wants more
but can't.

The stiffness stays.

The glass between the parlour
and the hallway is marked
with grease-stained hands
and smudges of
rain.

     * * *

The yellow school bus
waits.

Thieves

Daddy lifts
his fists and
knocks it against
mommy's cheek.

Brother tells me
I can't pee standing up.

Daddy he praises me
when I chop wood
and bring rabbits home
and hoe down weeds.

* * *

In mission school
the nuns cut my long hair
and cover me
in thick dresses.

When I shower
they cover my tits and my bum
take a scrub brush to my back.

That boy he corners me
and touches
my spoon and makes
me cry.

In church on my knees
I pray to father
about that dirty hole.

In the classroom
when I talk
when I write about the boosh
they laugh and scold me
make me stand in the corner.

And that girl
with thick lips
mean talk
her stick
scares me.

And that nun
in black robes
with prayer beads
makes me peel potatoes
makes me iron sheets
makes me polish the floors
and strips my lumpy bed.

* * *

I feel good with beer
drink the boys
wear make-up
and sexy clothes
show off my legs.

I travel to Jamaica
go to university
and laugh at that old
broken English.

I've dumped religion
and sit cross-legged in the
sweatlodge, chanting songs.

I've married   *well.*

Returning

It's raining, and the salt slides down my face into my mouth. Blue Quills Residential School, the log cabin. Memories. I summon them all.

I have been asked many times, wasn't residential school better than the fires that raged at home? I don't find that a fair question. My grasshopper legs clung only to the crippled love I came to know. It lay for years snared within the red walls of the residential school. Such shame. Such assault. That's what it was, refined under the rule of reading, writing, and arithmetic, and a god that had the eyes of a roving fly. This god wore black robes, cowls, and beads. Pebble beads, hard and polished as wind-swept rocks with silver and wood crosses where jesus died for my sins.

I grew up behind those walls. Six years. I knelt each morning in the chapel, up at dawn to pray to jesus to save my soul. I hoped that I would win an award for being the most pious, most committed at the end of the year. I can't help it when the buds between my legs tingle. I can't help it when my eyes stray to explore the tits of other girls. Why must I hide my body, jesus? The rags that I wear when I shower are so heavy, will I ever be clean? The scrub brush is not hard enough.

And jesus, can you tell me how to love a boy? I must not have such dirty thoughts or I will get purgatory and venial sin. I can't tell the priest in the confessional, so I write my sins and ask for penance.

At night I leave tears. I want my mother, my father, my brothers, my sister. I hold a sucker from my brother underneath my pillow. For weeks I take only a lick. I peek at my brothers across the dining room. I mustn't look too long. Why can't I look and talk to my brothers? At home during the laughing bloom of leaves we fight and cheat at our games. They call me ugly and flat chested. I hate them. In them I see my father, double tongues of laughter spinning my thoughts. Yet we work together and marvel at the wood stacked for our parents. We want to surprise them, but they never say a word. They too are the children of residential school. We know only how to show anger. We are always suspicious of one another. Watching, forever watching.

The little girls hate me. There is one with big lips assigned to the ruler. I hate her. She slaps us hard. We stand around the girl with white skin when its her turn to have her hair combed. One, two, three, ah, the numbers are too great. Lice. We are in awe, yet we shame her as she wins the count. At home my mother creams my hair with kerosene and I sit till all the bugs are dead. With gentle hands she pulls white nits. I listen to her murmur stories of *Wīsahkecāhk*. Her hands are two dead branches at her side when I leave for residential school. I see her next, when the pussy willows green. Her eyes will be bruised and black.

Father hands me the butcher knife and tells me to take over the skinning of the deer, but first he salts the fresh kidneys he's brought home. He never tells me, but I hear him brag that I'm a good little skinner. I never know when the thunder will burst, never know when the lightning will strike. My memories roll inside my stomach. Mean little butterflies at home, and at residential school.

The supervisor has huge keys hanging from her skirt. Everywhere we go she pulls her keys to unlock the stores of toilet paper, towels, Sunday morning tams. We are given three sheets of toilet paper. We learn to fold and refold. A hundred little squares of shit squeezed inside my heart. I didn't know I had locked away these memories, the keys jingling in the corridor of other people's stories.

I remember my first kiss. I received it on the staircase, treasured the feel of my first love's mouth for months. I didn't know what to do with him. Love was saliva, tongues of tobacco smoke, the hidden spirits.

Yet, when the life in my belly kicked and milk trickled down my breasts the mountains called. The sweet sweetgrass smoke and the sweatlodge rocks woke my spirit. I knew then where I was cradled.

der poop

der poop
forgive me for writing on dis newspaper
i found it in da outhouse, saw lines
dat said you is sorry
some of my indian friends say is good but
some of dem say you sorry don't walk
so i was sitting here dinking dat we
maybe dalk
say, i always want to dell you stay
out of my pissness
if me wants to dalk to trees
and build nests in house
dats hup to me
if me wants to pitch my dent
and feed da ghost bannock hen berries
and maybe drow some indian popcorn
for you geezuz dats hup to me
i don't hask forgiveness not want
hand mary's, or a step ladder to heaven
me is happy with da sky, da bird *Iyiniwak*,
four-legged *Iyiniwak*, i is happy
sorry mean dat i don't need yous church
and yous priest telling me what to do
sorry mean dat i free to dalk to Manitou
the spirits and plant *Iyiniwak*.
dats all for now, poop
maybe we dalk again next time i see you
in da newspaper.

Pâhkahkos

Flying Skeleton
I used to wonder where
You kept yourself.
I'd hear you rattle about
Scraping your bones

I opened a door
You grinned at me
Your hollow mouth
Stared through my heart
With empty eyes.

You lifted your boney hands
To greet me and I
Ran without a tongue.

You jumped on my back
Clinging to my neck you hugged
My mound of flesh.

For a thousand years you were
The heavy bones
The companion who would not leave.

You knocked your skull
On my head
I felt your boney feet.
I dragged and dragged
I couldn't carry
Your burden more.
I pried you loose
Bone after bone.

We stood, skull to face
Pâhkahkos, your many bones
Exposed
I, lighter than I could stand.

I fed you the drink of healing
You ran skeleton fingers
Down your face and onto mine.

I gave you a prayer cloth
I wove a blanket of forgiveness
You covered us both, skeleton and flesh.

I gave you the smoke of truth
You lit your Pipe to life
You lifted it to your ghostly mouth,
To mine.

My *Pâhkahkos* companion,
My dancing Skeleton
My dancing friend.

We carry our bundles
Side by side
Bones and flesh.

Nôhkom, Medicine Bear

A shuffling brown bear
snorting and puffing
ambles up the stairs.

In her den
covered wall to wall
herbs hang ... carrot roots, yarrow,
camomile, rat-root,
and *câcaâmosikan*.

To the centre of the room she waddles
sits with one leg out, the other hugged close.
She bends over her roots and leaves
sniffs, snorts and tastes them
as she sorts them into piles.

She grinds the chosen few
on a small tire grater,
dust-devils settling into mole hills.
Her large brown paws take a patch
of soft deer skin
and wraps her poultice
until hundreds of tiny bundle-chains
swing from the rafters.

The brown laboring bear
Nôhkom, the medicine woman
alone in her attic den
smoking slim cigarettes
wears the perfume of sage, sweetgrass
and earth medicine ties.

Nôhkom, the medicine bear
healer of troubled spirits.
A red kerchief on her head,
blonde-white braids hang below her breasts.
She hums her medicine songs
shuffling alone in her den where
no light penetrates, no secrets escape.

She bends and her skirt drapes
over her aged beaded moccasins.
She brushes the potions off her apron.
A long day's work complete
Nôhkom ambles down the stairs
sweeps her long skirt behind her
drapes her paws on the stair rails
leaves her dark den and its medicine powers
to work in silence.

Body Politics

Mama said,

Real woman
don't steal
from the sky and wear clouds
on their eyelids.

Real woman
eat rabbit well-done
not left half-raw
on their mouth.

Real woman
have lots of meat
on their bones.
They're not starving,
hobbled horses
with bony, grinding hips.

Real woman caress
with featherstone hands
not with falcon fingernails
that have never worked.

When she was finished talking
she clicked her teeth
lifted her arse
and farted
at the passing
city women.

Valentine Dialogue

I got bit.

By what?

A snake bite.

Where?

In my spoon. Gon er eeah.

Wholee sheeit.

Love he dold me.

I have a pain in my heart.

Fuckin liar.

Hate all of them.
Dink day can hang dair
balls all over da place.

Cross my legs next dime.

Mudder says day all alike.

Snake in dair mouth
snake in dair pants.
Guess dat's a forked dongue.

Mudder says I'll never lift it down.
Fadder says I'm nothin but a cheap dramp.

Shame, shame
Da pain in my heart hurts, hurts.

My brown tits
day shame me
My brown spoon
fails me.

Tired of sinning.
Dew ya dink confession will help?
Dew ya dink prayers will clean me?
Maybe I be born again.
Da pain in my heart hurts, hurts.

Durty priest
Jest wants da durty story
Needs to shine his rocks.

Fuckin men.

Day dink I a cheap badge
to hang on dair sleeve, as if
I an easy spoon.

A dongue in dair mouth.
A dongue in dair pants.
No nothin 'bout the heart.
No nothin 'bout my soul.

Day lookit my mouth.
Must be a nice mouth
cuz I see da look
in dair eyes.

And my mouth
wants
to feel dair wet lips.

It's mudder's fault
never told me right from wrong
Fadder's fault
always say mudder a slut.
Guess I must be one too.
Guess I showed dem.

Meet nice man one day.
Maybe brown.
Maybe white.
Maybe black.
Maybe yellow.

Won't show
my body talks.
Won't tell
'bout the snake bite.

pawâkan

Voice Dancer *pawâkan*, the Guardian of Dreams and Visions,
prayer, brings to you this gift.

> *Glory be to* okâwîmâwaskiy
> *To the* nôhkom âtayôhkan
> *To* pawâkan
> *As it was in the Beginning,*
> *Is now,*
> *And ever shall be,*
> *World without end.*
> *Amen. Amen.*

The walk began before I was a seed.

My mother strung my umbilical cord in my moccasins.

When I was a grasshopper *nimosôm* would open a big book. His
fingers traced the path of *cahkipêhikana* / ᐊᖠᒎᐃᐧᐅ, mouth
moving quietly.

Long after *nimosôm* died my memory went to sleep. I woke in the
mountain lying in the crook of my white husband's arms,
cocooned in the warmth of our teepee.

nimosôm took my fingers and guided me through his book.
Another old man sat in the grove of trees, lifted his Pipe, my
hands on the stem.

When I returned to the cabin I filled the pockets between the logs
with papers, stacked the walls with my books. A man, braids
hanging past his shoulders, laughed.

Still in my walks, the mountains beneath my feet, I picked feathers
as I climbed, the wolves gentle in their following. Soon the
mountain too had feet. I swam down her clear water and stood
naked beneath her falls.

Nearby, windburned fences enclosed crosses, their hinged grey
arms dangled. I heard screams and gunshot in the early dawn.

After the fierce weeping of thunder and mad dash of lightning, the robins danced with the drumming of the Little People. I woke as the brilliant ribbon of Northern Lights melted into a sunrise.

I was stuck, the weasel untangled my braids, ran down my heart while *nôhkom* sat at the foot of the bed, her weight shifting as she sang. I walked up the mountain again, loaded with gifts.

âstam, she said. She rubbed my eyes with her sweat and I saw her many faces.

Each face sat at the altar with one large eye.

We picked chokecherries, lips stained. Crushed them between the rocks.

In her cabin where *nôhkom* waited was a stoneboat stacked full of her belongings. Spotted blue enamel plates, oversize spoons, crazy quilts. She invited all my relatives to her feast.

She sang, her Voices echoing through the cabin. As I slept through the songs my hands became rocks too heavy to lift. Ants scurried in and out of the cracks, carrying crumbs, chewing bits of dirt, digging many holes. Eggs squirmed.

I'm awake now and remove my ring.

When I married him I dragged the cord past the road where my reserve ended.

ê-kî-âhtaskêyan, they said. I put my land elsewhere when I became his wife.

The prairie is full of bones. The bones stand and sing and I feel the weight of them as they guide my fingers on this page.

See the blood.

On my left breast was a hoofprint. It disappeared when I began the walk for them:

> okâwîmâwaskiy
> *full of grace,*

The Creator is filled with thee;
Blessed art thou among iskwêwak
and blessed is the fruit of thy womb,
Holy mother of all
Pray for us kitânisak,
now and at the hour
of our death. Amen.

Adeline Cardinal. Emma Woods. Sara Cardinal. Bella Shirt. Nancy
Gladue. Fanny Sunchild. Round Face Woman. Charlotte. Ah-gat.
Bernard Woman. Pray to them.

Glory be to okâwîmâwaskiy
And to nôhkom âtayôhkan

wâpâsôs – Up At Dawn Woman. Frying Pan Woman. Vera. Pauline
Johnson. Shawnidit. Waskedich Woman. Wet Pants Woman.
Carter Woman. Rubber Mouth Woman. Louiza. Ehnah — Sarcee
Woman. Pray to them.

And to pawâkan
As it was in the beginning.

Lightning Woman. McGuiness Woman. One Spot Woman.
Campbell Woman. Benson Woman. Sun Dog Woman. Rainy Bird
Woman. Windy Boy Woman. Small Woman. Stump Woman. Pray
to them.

Is now,
And ever shall be

Boudreau Woman. Lizzbeth. Large Woman. Rocky Boy Woman.
Cameron Woman. Clearwater Woman. Cuthand Woman. Good
Leaf Woman. Kingfisher Woman. Lameman Woman. Pray to
them.

World without end.
Amen. Amen.

Linklater Woman. Morin Woman. Many Fingers Woman. Martin
Woman. Minnie. Moosewah Woman. Kathleen. Pasqua Woman.
Shirt Woman. Carlson Woman. Pray to them.

okâwîmâwaskiy
who art in tawahikan
Hallowed be thy name

McGilvery Woman. Fiddler Woman. Cook Woman. Horse Dance
Woman. Russell Woman. Whitecloud Woman. Snake Woman. She
Flies Strong and Swift Woman. Yellow Knee Woman. Swiftwolf
Woman. Pray to them.

Thy Creation come
Thy will be done

Sitting Weasel Woman. She Has Strong Back Strong Wings
Woman. Bosivert Woman. Thompson's Mistress. Jobson Woman.
Factor Grant's Woman. Desjarlais Woman. Ross Woman. Kewin
Woman. Bear Woman. Pray to them.

asiskiy *as it is in* kîsik
Give us this day our daily reminders

Hamelin Woman. Wailing Woman. Sky Woman. Littlestick
Woman. *wâpawês* Woman. Black's Woman. Connolly Woman.
Dodging Horse Woman. Suzanne. Flora. Pray to them.

of sâkihitowin, *of* kisêwâtisiwin
And forgive us our shortcomings
As we forgive those who trespass against us

Big Heels Woman. Little Bear Woman. Night Traveller Woman.
cicîmân Woman. Trottier Woman. Ugly Face Woman. Little
Hunter Woman. Lone Woman. Crooked Neck Woman. Ballenden
Woman. Pray to them.

Oh mâmaw-ôhtâwîmâw
Lead us into Celebration

Buffalo Woman. Bear Hat Woman. Eliza. Mouse Woman.
Whistling Eagle Woman. Blackman Woman. Berland Woman.
McNeil Woman. *wâsatinaw* Woman. Quintal Woman. Pray to
them.

We give you thanks for the Four Legged.
The Winged People. The Swimmers.

Whiskyjack Woman. Rabbit Woman. Pond Woman. Blackfeather
Woman. Memnook Woman. lronman Woman. Fur-Trader's Wife.
First Wife Woman. Bone Woman. Thunder Woman. Pray to
them.

We give thanks to the piyêsiwak —
Whose voice sings from kîsik.

Callihoo Woman. A Bunch of Bitches Woman. Rolling Head
Woman – *cihcipistikwân.* Striped Gopher Woman. Wildman
Woman. Little Chief Woman. Badger Woman. Horse Woman.
Watchmaker Woman. Silver Cloud Woman. Pray to them.

We give thanks to the nôtokwêsiwak
We give thanks to the kisêyiniwak
The Keeper of the âcimowinis
nôhkom âtayôhkan

Sparkling Eyes Woman. Ermineskin Woman. Littlechild Woman.
Janvier Woman. Giant Woman. Youngchief Woman. Oaks
Woman. Squirrel Net Woman. Macleod *iskwêw.* Simpson's
Woman. Pray to them.

mâmaw-ôhtâwîmâw,
who art in tawahikan
Hallowed be thy name

McDougall Woman. Douglas Woman. McTavish Woman.
Matooskiie. Fraser Woman. Batoche Woman. Big Plume Woman.
Melting Tallow Woman. Big Stone Woman. Thanadelthur
Woman. Pray to them.

Lead us to Creation and
Deliver us into mâmitonêyihtêstamâsowin
into the matotisân

Bright Eyes Woman. Wander Spirit Woman. Damn You Woman.
Lip Pointing Woman. Baptiste Woman. Thunder Child Woman.

Sonnabitch Woman. Tallman Woman. Sky Dance Woman.
Crowfoot Woman. Pray to them.

> *For thou art the Parent of All, the connection,*
> *and the Centre, the Universe*
> *the power*

Cardinal Woman. Mud Hen Woman. Old Woman. Fire Thunder
Woman. Kicking Horse Woman. Big Swan Woman. *kâ-itwêhât* –
She Who Says So Woman. To all *nîci* Women. All my Relations.
Amen.

> *the glory*
> *Now and forever*
> *Amen. Amen.*

Grandmothers hold me.
I must pass all that I possess,
every morsel to my children.
These small gifts.

I sit by the window

I sit by the window
Thick woodsmoke lets the moon shine in.
I take my finger and walk it,
leave mice-size tracks.
The cabin is warm with the smell of bannock.
This long bone I hold
leaves me calloused and cold.
A few months ago I chewed all the meat
and now I've become clever.
I press these words hard
with charcoal
over and over
so I can write.
The little ones with dirty blond hair
look at me with dawn's eyes. I travel with them
into their backyard
where those men of god docked their ships,
took brown wives,
left them in barns and stalls —
horseflies and mosquitoes.
Many years have passed.
The moon our only eye,
it travels the silent roar of the lake,
the grand stillness of the rocks.
These blond children of the fur traders
seep through our women
even though they have long remarried
into the dark bark of our grain.
Their grandmother's chant cuts
the air on a dead drum,
"devil's spawn, devil's spawn."
Over the hills the bone climbs
slowly past the metal crosses
pounded in the ditches,
nailed hubcaps shine
in the centre of the holy bones.

Every dirt car rattling over this washboard road,
its braided passengers crossing themselves.
The sign of the cross is never holy.

A little red rose and lonesome charlie
spilled through the mud-stained windows
slur jesus' name.
They pass where someone saw
mary's radiance.
I see her myself, radiant, her bloody hands,
her bloody heart, her half-starved face.
She draws
till my head is a massive throb.

I am in this room.

A mosquito buzzes my arm.
I've smudged with sage.
I think repelling thought
for the mosquito and these icons.
My hunt is without a rifle,
without a net,
my bone
filled with the fists of women
of the fur trade.

The orange sunset dies
beneath broken beer bottles,
the birds cackle
in the embers of the dying heat.

I receive a rock in the mail.
Hummingbird sends a wing.
I barricade myself.
My fingers crows,
ravens the computer.
Quebec. Referendum.
I sip *okinîwâpoy*.
Chew *wîhkês*.
Notes slip under my door.
I can hardly get past my throat.

Large white splattering
at the House.
Feathered people storming.

Columbus wrote:
"*My wound has opened again.*"

His bones at the cathedral of Santa Domingo
moved four times,
different burial grounds.
In the last move his ashes
spill and are trampled.

Possession took me last night.
I slept with a bone.
The jawbone of elk lined with pearly teeth.
I bathed her in sweet grass. Laid her under my pillow.
Winds swept through me. This path has chosen me,
this chosen walk is a blizzard whiteout.
My Cree-ing alone in the heavy arm of snow.

I hang onto this bone
dressed in satin. Wade into redberry lakes.
I am married
to her garden of carrots and sweet corn heads.
I lay her skull, broken jaws,
face them to the East.

When *nôhkom*'s granddaughter slept
on top of graves
I thought she was crazy. All night I danced
above her head.
She dragged a string of skulls, heavy
in torrent rains. Cree-ing loud into my night.

I sleep with rocks too.
I couldn't say this before.
Who could I say it to except *nôhkom*'s granddaughter?
The rocks fill me. Their stories,
slates in dreams, heavy in my stomach,
move like thick clouds blown by my laboured breathing.
I cannot catch them.
I don't think to ask them
to slow down.

I sleep with petrified wood too.
Frozen snails, snakes with amber eyes,
crystallized tails.

Soon the black robes
will burn me,
stake me to their cross.
I won't have to live
in whiteouts much longer.

pê-nîhtaciwêk, nôhkomak.
pê-nânapâcihinân.
kwâhkotêw, nipônênân
pê-nîhtaciwêk, nôhkomak.
pê-nânapâcihinân.
ê-sôhkêpayik. kimaskihkîm.
kâ-wî-nânapâcihikoyâhk.
pê-nîhtaciwêk, nôhkomak.
kitimâkinawinân. sawêyiminân.

pê-nîhtaciwêk, nôhkomak.
Climb down, my Grandmothers.

pê-nânapâcihinân.
Come heal us.

The thick fog, the fog has lifted.
The ice shattered.

The crossing of the roads
is where we wait.

pê-nîhtaciwêk, nôhkomak.
Climb down, my Grandmothers.

pê-nânapâcihinân.
Come heal us.

ê-sôhkêpayik. kimaskihkîm.
Your medicine so powerful.

kâ-wî-nânapâcihikoyâhk.
That which will heal us.

pê-nîhtaciwêk, nôhkomak.
Climb down, my Grandmothers.

kitimâkinawinân. sawêyiminân.
Take pity on us. Bless us.

> *Bless me, father. I've pierced my flesh. Danced*
> *with the Sun. Bathed my face in blood.*
> *I didn't mean to.*
> *Forgive me, father. I ask for absolution.*
> *I promise to say my rosary and serve my time.*
> *I promise to keep my hands to myself and*
> *swallow my tongue. Amen.*

We gathered in a darkened room,
bodies pressed leg to leg. Our breath
mint and garlic, sage and sweet grass
woven into our burlap gown.
We held hands, my love and I.
On each side my mother and father sat
Blankets tea sugar flour gunpowder.
Tobacco ribbon blueberry cloth.
In the dark they came.

I bring to you
these Voices I will not name. Voices
filled with bird calls, snorting buffalo,
kicking bears, mountain goats.
I do not recognize who speaks.
Skin unfolds. Sag after sag.
Words squeezed through her
blistered tongues
lick till my heart stings, my
eyes swell.

Lightning flitted.
Scorched our flesh.
They tore out our tongues.

When we spoke,
my love and I, darkness swelled.
Thunder became our footsteps. This
ceremonial dance of my dead.
We were wedded that night.
The night has no shadow,
her veil always an open mouth.
Listen to the bones.

nôhkom âtayôhkan

> The Keeper of the Sacred Legends – *nôhkom*
> *âtayôhkan*

For centuries
I've tumbled through thistles,
charcoal stars and suns,
groaning lakes and rivers,
my hairy skull
a home for mice and snakes.

A cursed man
chopped up my body,
sent my sons running. Now he swims
in stars,
me dangling in his fist.

I'm earth
born each moon,
waxing and waning,
bleeding eggs.

I'm painted red on rocks;
I swim the caves in lakes
where my head sinks
and I drink to roll again.

The boys have been running.
They are old and wrinkled hearts.
They've eaten leathered flesh.
Knuckles gnawed to the bone,
they run.

The medicines they've thrown
to thorn my path
I've gathered, the Bundles
given to amisk *– beaver,* iskotêw *– fire*
and the swan.
They run from their mother's
nursing tongue.
The flaming open womb,

the burning boiling bone
rolls round and round in
the hairy head.

nâpêsisak, *wailing coyotes,*
run the river bends,
cast your medicines!
nâpêsisak, *wailing boys,*
dust swirls beneath your feet.
The tribal bones
and swimming moon
will fly.

Forgive me father

Forgive me father; I have sinned. I have hauled these
tongues of iskwêwak *since 1492. I no longer know*
which of me speaks.

There were times, nôsisim,
my heart wanted to stop seeing.
I spooned wîhkês – *med-sins into my sister.*
She lay on the ground
filled with homebrew.
Snot covered her baby's moccasin.
The year omikiya – *scabs*
tracked us.

When the snow fall
her spirit go.

I Thirst Dance,
Ghost Dance,
Track Dance,
Chicken Dance,
I Give-Away Dance,
Beaver Dance,
Owl Dance,
Beg Dance.

My moccasins chewed those dances.
My heart gorged. My thoughts slaughter.

kahkiyaw iskwêwak, nôtokwêsiwak, câpânak,
êkwa ohkomipanak.
Grandmothers, and the Eternal Grandmothers wail
in unison

sôhkêyimo. sôhkêyimo
pimâtisi. âcimostawinân.

Strive in boldness. Strive in strength.
Live.
âcimo.

âcimowinis

Smoke shrouds the dried meat
hanging on a tripod. The sun dips.
She shifts. I puff small winds.
Knee-deep in earth, fingers clawing,
head bobs up and down.
She is there. She is not. A dog howls.

I am câpan, *the grandmother who shamed her family
when sound choked me. Bless me father, this is my sin.*

*I watched my people hunched
under their belongings,
worn-out pots, pans clanking:
Babies wailing or asleep in cradle boards.
Bony dogs pulling their travois.
I hear the buffalo hoofs pounding
in their stomachs.*

Our men's faces grim,
braids fraying, hair in mud.
Only the young bucks strode,
jaws set for the rising sun.

âcimowinis

and we barricaded them.

It was not the only time
I hated the man
whose white flesh
shared my bed.
My memory snared
by my people, beggars in the land
that once filled their bellies.

I still see those
Grandmothers clench the Bundles,
whisper songs through the night.

câpân, Grandmother, continues strangling, an
umbilical cord tied her to the earth.

I'd steal flour, sugar, tea,
pass it to my children late at night.
My efforts received by
swollen tongues.
I hung
my husband's twine on
lone tree.

âcimowinis

In the arbour twilight mouth
flags bend, eagles whistle.

The Sky Dancers circle
my head.

kahkiyaw iskwêwak, nôtokwêsiwak, câpânak, êkwa
ohkomipanak.
Grandmothers, and the Eternal Grandmothers
murmur

Squirrels, tall pines, cones, moss.
The jesuits ask do you believe in soul.
When wolves howl, I descend into his mouth.
When coyotes pluck prairie chickens.
I fill his belly. Terra Nullius. *Amen.*

âcimowinis

My words get in your way.
I feel your sting.
My printer refuses to feed my leaves.
A squirrel stakes out
the sink.
I feed him my apple.
My printer sins.

Father, these robes I wear confuse me. I have forgotten
who I am. a jesuit. A monk. A brother. A priest. A
nun, perhaps. It matters not. I have sinned. My last
confession was in 1492. Yesterday. Ah yes, late today.

I wrote his Eminence,
offered my life to save savage souls.
My mother kissed my crucifix,
said, God go with you.

I am filled with wind, empty forest,
savages peek beneath my robe,
tender hands send heat up my spine.
I bless them.

The whip doesn't bite hard enough, Mother.
I crouch under the cross. Shroud my face.
Swallow. Swallow. Swallow.

This salt water I trickle,
send the Father's Bible thundering.
God be with you.

These savage men – they laugh at my disdain
of their brown-breasted women.
I grind the crucifix. Dry myself.
God be with me.

kahkiyaw iskwêwak, nôtokwêsiwak, câpânak, êkwa
ohkomipanak.
The Grandmothers, and the Eternal Grandmothers
proclaim

There are Holy iskwêwak *–* nôsisim, *all over.*
We were the ones who burned down the jesuits'
church, trilled, danced and laughed through the night.
We watched those cabins eaten by our flames. We
were the ones, nôsisim, *who hid the Bundles,*
held council when we learned how those brothers

lifted their skirts to spill their devils into our sons' night.
And did they think they suffered as they burned,
screaming against our flame?

nôhkom âtayôhkan

I am weary
Snakes dance above my head.
Spit from my womb.
Entwine my legs.
I am not done.

âcimowinis

Sage Woman Eyes with Spirits.
When Thunder speaks,
Lightning flashes from them.
I sit with her in her Lodge.
We cling to our Pipes and weep.
When we weep her tears get up,
become Blue Butterflies.
Mine become Little People
beating their drum.
Butterflies dance.
The Morning Robins lay
their heads to one side
then to the other.
Lift their bustles,
War Dance around our Lodge.
Neither one of us wants to brush away
our tears.

kayâs-âcimowin nôtokwêsiw wîhtam

kayâs-âcimowin nôtokwêsiw wîhtam
Wandering Stone Grandmother mouths a corn pipe
pokes holes in heavy smoke circles as she speaks

I've been carrying these little rocks.
My bundle heavy.
I've waited long to move them,
rumbling and roaring,
chipping and polishing
till they've become stones
I cannot lift.

I started collecting
the year I first laid eyes
on the white flesh.
He lay his body on mine.

The seasons are many, each stone
pressed into my flesh.
Sharpen the bone,
pierce my temples, suck till the stones
bleed. They've lain
heavy, so heavy. Too long.

môniyaw-kisêyiniw, an Old Pelt Man rubs
weatherworn hands down his thin wool pants,
and ejects his dreams.

I wanted her
I took her.
My stirring
hovered her mouth.

Wandering Stone Grandmother swallows

This little stone, its heart beats beneath my head.
She sings Chinooks
to break the ice inside my gut.

I place the stone in a bowl of water,
stirred all night while cinders danced.
At dawn, our bellies full,
we crossed âyimani-sîpiy – Difficult River,
energy in our thighs,
laughing at the stumbling redcoats.

> *môniyaw-kisêyiniw,* the Old Pelt Man kicks against
> an invisible shore, birchbark canoe wrecked in his
> memory

I arrived at the new world sent by the King,
chained and flogged.
I didn't know I'd flee,
the law against my back.
This country where I found my worth.
The savages led me through the valleys.
Promised them whiskey
I'd mix with chewing tobacco, ginger, red pepper,
molasses and a dash of red ink
enough to fill their thirst.

Her, don't believe a word she says.
She's just a toothless squaw
who laid with me after her father died.

> Wandering Stone Grandmother weeps her prayer

This stone dropped from my eye.
His fist spoke after my tongue clawed
about the water that caused our men
to spread our thighs, their tongues knives,
vomiting the night.
This stone, its small belly
weighed my infant at Whirlpool Point.
My breasts slaughtered bags
of sweet wine.

> *môniyaw-kisêyiniw* – Old Pelt Man roars

I've no love for girl-childs.
Her mouth's too small, I stifled her yawns,
made my squaw tie her cord.
My squaw. We bucked the night, skins
filled. It's been so long since I've had a woman.
The young boys no longer need to trade.
Her thin legs, tight hold of her buttocks.
I whip, slap till foam drips.
Strange taste of her. I try to be gentle with my
greedy squaw. Fill her
with British blood.

Wandering Stone Grandmother wails.
Voice drifts and bites hard snow.

I was not always cold, tight in heart.
I was not always roped in his fist.
My .22 shot rabbit, grouse, robins,
filled the moment's hunger.

This stone, its white-veined forks
mark the day
my spirit and I
become this stone,
head bowed too heavy to lift.

I was the open flap to all his trades,
my legs unable to walk.
And when he lifted his axe while I slept
my spirit had already gone.

Born in a Dent Grandmudder

Born in a Dent Grandmudder stutters her story

Our feet were free
Before da walk of da white skin.
I can't dell you where I waz born.
In a dent somewhere,
maybe in da bush. Mudder
squat an push.
The wind – yôtin
scream and scream.
But not Mudder.

My mudder and fadder were liddle bid Irish
an French. My grandfadder, dough, he dick
dough white skin speak grandmudder's Cree.
She, grandmudder, was a pure. I 'member dere
stories. You grandfadder he dell you first.

Old Grandfather Trader he want her he speaks

I was a French lad
used to ramble boat to boat.
Little chore here, little chore dere,
earn me livin', wine, women.
I'd live on pork. I work ard,
got my hands to show it.

Everytime we turn a corner 'round dem lakes da land stop
my breating. Over each ill we climb, god's and stretch more
dan our eye can see. Old Woman's Lake. Where the Moose Died.
Dried Meat ills. I pull my rosary an dunk da god for dem sky
an ills. Swear da devil when we suffer from wads of mosquito,
sandflies, noseeums, horseflies. Somedime go hungry for days.
Plenty animals but our hunters waz clomping trough dem woods
scare da by jezuz outta da mooze. Da savages waz good to us.
Drezz in dem furs an skins an hide, faces paint. Not one fat savage,
dough can't say any one of us waz ever in lard. I see many
change in my dime.

Dem jezuits had it in dem to make dat savage holee, didn't like
dere wild chantin', smokin' dem grazz an makin' der mozez
speakin' to dem bushes an round rocks. I'm little blind now
but I still see kôhkom, *in dat water hole. Didn't no I was*
watchin'. Maybe snare me like a rabbit if she no. We'd sneak.
Dey had eyes like hawk, ears like wolf, but we use deze long
stalk wit large eye. I see trough them willow. Yes. My man
want her. I not a rich fellow in dem days but I work hard
had me some cheraux, i dired of sewin' me own hide,
dired of me cold bedroll, my cabin could use fresh bannock
an smell of woman. Never mind she greaze wit animal lard,
make it eaze for trappin'. An doze elk teeth she wear on
her breast, well dat's all right too.

Born in a Tent Grandmother *kiskisiw*
Her memory stirs

Yes, kimosôm, *his doughts dake many paths,*
memory full. Liddle string died to dat liddle string.
I dravel wit him, crossed dat sôhkêciwani-sîpiy.
Dere we watch butterfly swallows. Swarms an swarms
makin' a blanket of tiger lily. He said dem old savages
use to dell him fellow like im a lonesome warrior.
Dey cry for der nîcimos, *an der* nîcimos *woman*
would dance trough dat butterfly flower. Dere earts
would sing, dey no dere woman is safe an soon dere
finger meet. I dought dat somedime soon I see
nîcimos *sing love song in dem trees across da river.*
When we stand by dat swollen stealin river an da
butterfly dance, we no to paddle soft an swift.

Keeper of the Stories

Keeper of the Stories – *âcimowinis*

They hobbled, limped, shuffled,
pink, purple, blues, reds, yellows,
white, black, printed blazed
calico dresses, shawls,
kerchiefs, blankets.
Dried flowers, old sweat
and sweet perfume, they teased,
laughed, joked and gossiped.
Ran their fingers through each
swinging hand. Pipe smoke
swirled. Men drumming our songs.

I watch them. Hundreds of my husband's family.
They've travelled across Canada, the United States,
rejoice at recognizing one another, some for the first time.
Each has brought a book they've lovingly compiled.
It contains the history of their migration
from England, Norway, and into the Dakotas.
They are scattered throughout Turtle Island.
They marvel at the trek of their ancestors.
The click of wine glasses echoes through the arbour
of this large family gathering. And five Indians.
I the eldest, my children and two other Indian youth.
They are not yet aware how this affects their lives.
Who are we? Adopted. I gather inward.
How many of my relatives were cattled
onto the reservation during their settlement?
How much of my people's blood was spilled
for this migration? Laughter and wonder
as fingers move across the atlas. This is where
great-granddad Arne crossed on the barge.
This is where great-great-granddad travelled
and preached the law of the land where his
wife Isobel taught the little savages to read.
My lips are tight from stretching when my
small family is introduced alongside the
large extended family. Later,
driving home, I weave a story for my children –

how their great-grandma rode sidesaddle,
waving her .22 in the air trying to scare
those relatives away. I tell them
how my relatives lived around the fort,
starving and freezing,
waiting for diluted spirits
and handouts from my husband's family.
I tell them
how their little children died wrapped in
smallpox blankets.
My breath
won't come anymore.
I stare
at the wheatfields.

Ram Woman

Ram Woman, we met for the first time.
You stood on top of graves at White Rabbit,
large eye staring.
My legs wrapped my husband.
Your head thumped those stones.

Ram Woman, I stood naked
beneath the falls.
Your hoofs pounded
in that April rain. I remember
your fist in your mother's womb,
heels kicking her door.
When her lips split
two birds flew
from your mouth. You
lifted your moccasins
in a Ghost Dance.
While the drummers sang
dogs ran after your meat
and bones, pissed at your feet.
You let them in. They left
nickels and dimes.

Ram Woman, always in pursuit
of the laughing sun,
the pregnant moon.
A gorging river, you plunge
heedless into the spring fire.
You drag your laughing, weeping
child in a trail of snares, shutting
out the wind.

Ram Woman, Ram Woman
in Kootenay Plains you sang,
lured me to your grave,
gave my heart a twist and
sent me flying, gave me
your large eye
for my stepping stone.

She came in a Vision, flipped many faces.
Stone-aged wrinkled, creased like a stretched drum,
thin flesh, sharp nose.
When the Sun sleeps she takes faded rays,
dresses her gown. She's the burnt rose of autumn,
a blue-winged warbler. The awakened river
flanked in every woman, rolling pebbles
over and over till stone eggs are left.
I travel with her youth, this Night Mistress.
Hair fresh, sweet grass braided in perfection.
Long ago Grandmother danced in glades,
women crushed chokecherries, saved the blood,
cleaned porcupine quills,
weaved them into birch baskets, chewed sinew.
They drummed, danced, lifted their dreams.
Ribboned the Sky.
Raw-boned,
they left their blood.
In these moccasin gardens
I pick my medicines.

I talk to Magpies. Their eyes my Womanhood.
How can I mark that?
The first ecstasy of climax?
Each squealing baby?
When told to cross my legs at ceremony?
When told never to walk over men when I was in
Full Moon?
Or was it the first time I gave away all my jeans,
sexy dresses and wore tents for a year?

Did our Grandmothers know we would be scarred
by the fists and boots of men?
Our songs taxed,
silenced by tongues that speak damnation and burning?
Did they know we would turn woman against woman?
Did they know some of us would follow,
take mates of colour and how the boarding of our worlds
would pulse breathing exiles connected to their womb?
Did they know only some would dig roots, few hands
calloused from tanning? Did they know only a few
would know the preparation of moose nose, gopher,

beaver-tail feasts? Did they know our memory, our
talk would walk on paper, legends told sparingly?
Did they know of our struggling hearts?

Each month Grandmother waxes and wains,
pregnant with wolverine and baying dog.
I become heat at Midnight,
a yowling cat, fingers stained. Quills.
Mark these songs.

We are Star People.
wîsahkêcâhk sang to the Water People
to bring back Earth from where we dove.
She pinched the mud from the exhausted Muskrat.
Blew *yôtin*. Blew *iskwêw*. *iskwêw* was born.
pimâtisiwin fills woman.
Man is born.

I return to the Moon glade,
turn up the sod,
lift up my songs.

Dream,
Grandmother dances at Midnight.
Grandmother Moon,
my Shadow
dreams the dark.

Grandmother, the Woman in me.

A pagan. Again.

All my relations. *ahâw*.

Listen: To the Story

We lived in tents, teepees before the four walls,
before the ugly, broken years.
Ears witnessed this story my mother, *aspin*,
unfurled.

aspin sat on a feathered buckskin blanket,
fingers bent willows. She dipped in the pail for red-stained
roots, her voice rising, falling, smoke curled toward the teepee's arms.
Fire crackled in front of her.

> kayâs êsa ... *Long, long ago our people were filled with mystery
> and unexplainable powers* ... ê-ki-mamâhcâwisicik.

We listened, skewered.
Waited long for this night.
Waited for the river to wear her ice-suet clothes.
Waited to wear our snowshoes, and track rabbits.
Waited. Waited.

The story gnawed, teased our infinite heavens.
The strawberry veins wrapped and nestled our hearts,
this Rolling Head. *cihcipistikwân.*

> kayâs êsa. *A man and a woman left the main camp
> with their two boys. They travelled, travelled, travelled,
> thick into the forest, thighs sucked in muskeg.
> The family fed the mosquitos.
> They gathered blue and cranberries, pin and bunch berries,
> mushrooms, rosehips, mint and muskeg.
> Juncos, chickadees, nuthatches, and whisky-jacks flew, scolding.
> Squirrels hoarded pine cones and hazelnuts. In the thicket
> bear, moose, elk and deer watched. The family
> pitched their skin tent upon a promise
> of birth and aspen syrup, spruce needle chews. A creek
> sang itself into a gorged lake. Here shadows waved.*
>
> sâkâstêw *peeled the night cloud, stretched into daylight.
> The man gathered his hunting tools, bannock and rabbit.
> He was gone all day.*

pahkisimotâhk *curled into the darkness*
and pulled up her night blanket.
The man returned.
Supper unmade. Wood untouched. His wife's
tanning undone.

aspin took a swig of tea,
poked the embers, studied her basket.
Our moccasins slipped into our ears.
We sat. Tongues possessed. We learned how to feed
the sky dancers *wiyin*, fat,
in the owl dance of their death.
Drums and songs beckon them to rise
and give them form.

aspin crumbles a tobacco leaf, lifts it,
feeds the fire. Her voice guttural,
wind silent, flames creep, fix the air with small stares.

The man asked the boys what they did all day.
The thoughts wrestled, twisted out: "Mother feeds us
and scolds never to follow her, she gives us work."
Mouths pointed to the forest.

For days the father shadowed his wife's movements. One day
she sat on a large log. Sang. Fist drummed.

A snake slithered out
followed by small snakes, excited tails flipping,
squirmed under her warm hands. This he watched.
Hard.

He filled his bundle; tobacco, stone axe, arrows and bow.
Gave his sons an awl, a flint, a rock, a beaver's tooth.
Told his sons the medicine's secrets
to be used only when the sky was red.

One day the man rose before the sun,
he drummed the log. The man bellowed.
His axe sliced the heads off each snake.
At camp, his wife still asleep,

he boiled broth, offered her the soup.
Her lips smacked thankful for the food.

Our bellies became a storm of worms.
We scratched our skulls, hair strands fell into our infinite heavens.
aspin's voice a drumstick against our ears,
stopped as we struggled to untangle her net.
She drank tea, gulping slowly, pushed
sweet grass into the embers. The wind
settled in her chest.

> *The woman shrieked, her lover trickling down her mouth.*
> *The sky bled, the husband severed her head, and*
> *cast her body to the heavens and he too ascends,*
> *his body the milky way. Her body dressed in streaks*
> *of green, purple, pinks, pale yellows – the bursting veins*
> *become the sky dancers. The head rolled, weeping.*
> *In the distance the boys watched. When the sky darkened*
> *they ran, bundles bouncing.*

aspin tucked us into a buffalo robe,
brushed our cheeks with stained hands. We strained
to see the rib-boned bodies where the heavens explode.
I, *ê-kwêskît*, thought if I ate a passing star
a womb nest of Shakers would love again.

Gone-For-Good's fingers ate spirits and danced.
wâpistikwân built a log-shack of mud and straw.
We lived on rabbit fetuses when *aspin*'s blackness
filled her. White Hair courted snake-hair
truths, they drank from piss-filled bottles. Sold
all our horses, cattle. Lost
our land. Ukrainians hired us to pick sticks
and stones and put up stooks.

Three Person, Mechanic, *ospwâkan*, I, *ê-kwêskît*, *wâpan*,
lost our bundles, wandered the maggot streets,
collected toys from throw away sites. Courted beneath
blankets behind bars.

Three Person made fatherless babies.
They fought for her dangling breasts

and learned to hate men with bad breath.
Mechanic became a stingy recluse,
chopped the tongues off his wives,
his children caged to his pelvis.

ospwâkan hovered at the tree line,
his crooked smile on his sons' lips.
Once in a billion stars we get a glimpse.

I, *ê-kwêskît*, and *wâpan* married white-skinned men,
babies held to our nursing breasts. Rib Woman returned.
Rolling Head gave us her bundles. Slowly
aspin's words unrolled.

wâpan buried Rolling Head and the serpents.
Rosary wrapped around Rib Woman,
she ghost danced, beg danced, guilt danced.
Her strawberry crucified.

Still the story followed.

     kayâs êsa …

And I, *ê-kwêskît* …
At dawn I slipped on thin shoes—
check my rabbit snares,
ask the chickadees, the snow, the sky
if I filled my being with her breath
would I be butchered too? Would I give chase to
what my loins delivered? Would I be spurned?
I kiss the stiff rabbits, throw them over my shoulder.
I peel their fur, wrap them on aspen. My belly full, I
remember the story.

     kayâs êsa ê-kî-mamâhtâwisicik iyiniwak. *Long, long, ago*
     the people were filled with mystery and magic.

aspin puffed on her pipe.

     The head wept. Sang. Rolled. Bumped along
     the trodden trails. Their home eaten by fire, flames leaped,

raced toward her. In the distance the boys heard their
mother's terrible cry. They ran. Ran. Ran.

Hearts raced. Wind burned throats.
Bones bent and stretched. Their mother's breath
at their heels.

I, *ê-kwêskît*, my finger's raced around
the pole, rabbit skin flying.
Eyes dart to fingers, to Gone-For-Good.
Where was I to sleep this night?
aspin's voice was sheets of forest rain,
leaves baking in the ragged wind.

"âstamik pê-kîwêk. *Come home. Come home.*
I love you my babies. My babies. My sons."
The head begged. Their father's wrath
coiled, held them to their gut. Icy fingers threw
their father's awl. Thorns, rosehips brush,
thistles, brambles, burrs sprung and crowned
the Rolling Head. Hair caught, tangled in these claws.
Rolling Head wept. She struggled, ripped
her face, gouged her eyes. She called. Called.
Still the boys ran, ran, ran.
A fox trotted by, heart filled by the Rolling Head's
wail. He led her through the pass. She rolled. Rolled.
Rolled. "âstamik nipêpîmak. nikosisak." Her voice
bee-shit sweet. Still the boys ran.

aspin took a twig. Relit her pipe.
Saw the story clench my eye,
saw *wâpan*'s inward look.
aspin began….

With severed breath she sang,
"nikosisak, nipêpimak. *Come home to your mother's hearth.*"
The eldest boy threw a flint. Fire sprung behind them.
Rolling Head's face, blistered bacon.
Hair a burnt trail scorched the summer soil.
Her breath a wind of flames at her sons' heels.
Gasping the eldest son turned again. Threw

the rock. Mountains, rocky hills, steep crevices, ravines rose.
She bayed, bayed, bayed.
Rolled back and forth. Back and forth.

I, *ê-kwêskît*, remember how mother, *aspin*, Gone-For-Good,
shot our twenty-two into the sky
whenever she heard a coyote bark, an owl hoot.
Our ears listened for those
creatures of the snowy dark.

aspin slid her hands
down *wâpan*'s face,
paused against my cheek.

    Oh the chase, so long, so long.

In teepee, dirt-floor cabin, in the city
the story followed. My memory sniffs
the woven trail.

Gone-For-Good padded the earth,
lifted arms toward the teepee's mouth.
Snowflakes drifted through the parted skin.
She sang for the Rolling Head,

    "My babies. My babies. My sons. My little sons.
    Come home. Come home. Come home
    to your mother's heart."
    The boys bled, moccasins eaten by their run.
    Bellies empty, eyes swollen, they limped.
    Still a beaver's tooth flew, a great river formed.
    The boys walked, bellies rolled with water.
    They gave themselves to the night.
    Across the lake Rolling Head promised
    a large water bird marriage if she would spread
    its wings. The Swan commanded her to stay still
    during the ride or her lonesome bones would
    collapse and they would drown.

aspin droned. I, *ê-kwêskît*, my Big Heavens
strained, I straightened my rabbit pole,
laid the fur aside. The skins would be a quilt.

The head clung. Crushed the swan's back. The bird
screeched, flopped and flipped the Rolling Head.
Deep, deep into the black depths, the Rolling Head
became a sturgeon. It flips its tail fin
and devours the river's rotten flesh.

wâpan and I, *ê-kwêskît*, nodded,
sank into the waiting robe.
We did not hear *aspin*'s final words.

In sleep this is where we go.

The embers are starlight
in memory's cave.

ê-kwêskît – Turn-Around Woman

When I was growing up in the bush, on the hillside,
I watched the sun arrive from the dark, watched her slip
into the dark. I travelled. I didn't know the world back then.
I just travelled. I was afraid
I would never return. I tumbled that hillside
back into myself.

You can tell me
after you hear this story
if my name suits me.
I've yet to figure it out.

In Rib Woman
stories are born.
The Old Man called it psychology. Me,
I just dream it.

> *These gifted mysterious people of long ago,*
> kayâs kî-mamâhtâwisiwak iyiniwak,

my mother, Gone For Good, would say.

> *They never died. They are scattered here, there,*
> *everywhere, somewhere. They know the language,*
> *the sleep, the dream, the laws, these singers, these healers,*
> âtayôhkanak, *these ancient story keepers*

I, Turn-Around, am not one of them.

I was taught by Old people.
An Indian Man, a White Man.
An Indian Woman, a White Woman.
They worked in lairs, in the full veins of
Rib Woman.

I sat in their thicket, wailing.
The old ones navigated through my dreams.
Sometimes they dragged, scolded, cajoled,

cheered and celebrated.
I wanted to be with them. Like them.

I am not a saint. I am a crooked good.
My cousins said I was easy, therefore
I've never been a maiden.
I am seventy, but still
I carry my sins. Brothers-in-law
I meet for the first time wipe their hands
as if I am still among the maggots. I didn't
know their women wept when their men
slept in my bed. I am not a saint.

I married Able, a wide green-eyed man. Fifty years now.
Inside Rib Woman I shook hands with promise.
Promise never forgot, trailed me year after year.
His Big Heavens a morning lake
drowns me in my lair.
I learned how to build Rib Woman
one willow at a time, one skin at a time.
I am only half done. This is part of the story.

I, *ê-kwêskît*, am a dreamer.
I dream awake. Asleep. On paper.
The Old Man said the universe,
the day, was the story. So,
every day I am born.
The Old White Man taught me
to unfold night visits.
The Old Woman taught me
all of it was real.
The Old White Woman helped me
To cry with the thunder.

The Tracker

A guitar strums,
fingers caress the chords.
Ears listen. The musician walks the alley.
I met him. I was bending into the wind.
Ice glares. He hears my sobs.
Lifts my hood, kisses my cheek.
The twang shatters the window,
frost spreads like fire rolling in snow.
The music is rhythmical. Hair falls on
his forehead …

> I am sad for all that has happened. This fire
> leaves a crater too deep to fill. Tell me what to do,
> ê-kwêskît, tell me what to do. You've torn my skin.
> I am a narrow miss in the traffic, still trembling.
> I am a slow learner as I go.

My room is filled with unruly books.
I watch him watching me as I drop my clothes.
Scars on my belly. Waist wattled,
swaddled, spills. I don't hide anything.

His murderous want to possess me.
He deposits my decapitated head in plastic,
wraps my limbs in a brown bag.
Brings me to a barn, lays me in a freezer.
Marked as hamburger.

I memorize his moves. Know his mouth.
His thoughts. His feelings. His doings.

I suffer Beloved too.
He moves next to me, snores in my ear.
I clasp his bum.

Romantic fever runs in my family.
Men's. Women's.
A catching disease.
Too many years of grieving

in Rib Woman, Rolling Head laughing.
I am surrounded by shakers in
this mud-water.

Rolling Head is hookworm.
I regurgitated her when I was snowshoeing.
Snow woman shifted between skins.
Her face ghostlike, nun cropped hair,
hips gyrating, she thrust her mound.
I dipped my finger.

Everyday Is a Story

Outside my window stands a rust-orange needled tree.
Beneath it is a pine, branches with thick spikes.
They stand aloof. Sure-footed. On my bed lie three binders,
bellies ink-filled. They wait. My stomach talks. I am hungry
for voice, though I live in terror. Unsure what shape will arrive.
Voices in thought. A wish. A desire. A dream. A vision.
Fingers cannot catch their passing. Invisible Little People.
I am deaf though my ear strains. Perhaps it is a crazed beast
that buys a two-bit Stetson at a garage sale. But
it's just mother *aspin*, Gone-For-Good, though she is
anything but gone.

    aspin wears tams, a kerchief now and then, a loose sweater,
    a v-neck dress whose waist is directly below her breasts. She sews
    her dresses, same shape if fat layers or hunger arrives.
        Garters hold up
    thick stockings, or cut-off ribbed socks at her ankles, and
    moccasin rubbers. Her money stashed in small purses,
        she says she
    is always broke. Then flashes her bank book.
    Gone-For-Good buys our strawberries, lures us with money
    and spits it out to watch the dog fight.
    But I, *ê-kwëskît*, am ahead of my story.

I am inhaling mountains.
Voices skate, flow beneath ice shelves, grope through cracks
to catch each breath, freeze the voice to itself. A duck
splayed in ice still flying, its voice racing beneath slivers.
Voices from nose-blowing ravens, they grind sputum
beneath their heels, curious beady heavens crane, peer.

    Female voices. Male. My husband's voice winds,
    wraps around my body. Deeply patient, fevered, his slender
    mouth an "O" of wet kisses. His voice a prayer lifting off a lake,
    broad as a tree trunk, moves as an infant's finger.
    He is woodsmoke, grassfire soot, grapefruit,
    a writing paper, a song in the sweat lodge. A stake
    in Rib Woman.

I build this story like my lair. One willow,
a rib at a time. Bent it into my hip, grounded into earth.
I walked the forest, hitchhiking seeds clung to my socks,
hopped into my pant cuff, bedded into the swollen lips
of my boots.
I walked slow, held a bucksaw, an axe.
Bled the willows, draped skins, hide, blankets, tarps
over their crippled bodies – this book took shape.
In this lair I lived in darkness. Dug a pit, heated
the grandfathers, till they sweated. Dreams dripped
from my breasts, from my many lips.

Have I told you where I grew up?
On a knoll, in a clearing. A small reserve called
wîhtikow sâkahikan, there they burned the flesh eater on ice.
That is another story.
We were divided by a creek, many hills,
cabins ruled by men. *aspin* and the rest
of the wives. Kept women. Even *nôhkomak*.
We competed with one another.
Stole. Shunned one another. Everyday events.
We were all saints.

> *aspin*, Gone-For-Good, the cream-butter belly, the fat eater
> lived when travel was horse and wagon.
> > She stayed in the Ukranian
> farmer's granary until *wâpistikwân* built her a log cabin.
> They owned a pickup. She never learned to drive.
> > They drove to
> *manawânis* – where cowboys and Indians gathered,
> > to town, to residential school to visit us.
> They stooked, picked rocks and roots.
> > Shovelled manure,
> worked in sugar beet fields. Janitored in sick buildings.
> > They drifted.
> Woods. Mountains. Back to *wîhtikow sâkahikan*.

Three-Person, Mechanic, *ospwâkan*, I, *ê-kwêskît*, *wâpan*,
we inherited laughter, mule skulls, working hands. None
escaped *pâhkahkos*. We travelled on brooms,

jalopies, luxury cars, airplanes, trains, ships.
We covered great distances. We all had loves. Secret loves.
Snake-tongued lovers. *aspin* believed in medicines.
Three-Person and Mechanic were like her. My medicine
came from the Old Men, the Old Women, I have no roots,
no herbs. Just
Dreams.

No one expected us, the brown-skins, to get anywhere.
Especially us women.

Excavating

I, *ê-kwêskît*, share this story,
though a small pain only.

Shadow dancers arrived, ran on Rib Woman's
roundness. Twigs fall. Thunder rolls. A
dead tree slaps Rib Woman. She
heaves through the night. Breathes, breathes.
Hours. Hours. Many, many nights.
Years. Years. Time and time again.
Rolling Head dreams. Mouth parched.
Tongue thick.

Obsession. Obsession. Obsession.
Over and over I leave him here.
Friends, that is all.
My rock has four heads
I found at Holy Lake. I smudge, cradle,
and sleep with it. This is my Beloved,
our children. I show my want.
A treaty. Yes, a treaty.
Still
hungry heavens bend, breathe me.
Knees stagger from this whorish inflammation.
He walked away from another. He doesn't
reveal names. I know, say her name.
A storm, red, black flushed. I've gone too deep.
Inheritance at work.
Swallow this bitter root.

ê-kwêskit 'awâsis êkwa nôtokwêsiw'

I am old. Old.
I've devoured my eggs
every mating moon. Lost my memory,
nôhkom drove me crazy. Sleepless nights,
she becomes Tammy Wynette, sings

> *"You're the reason I don't sleep at night,"*

leaves me with belly aching laughter.
I want to tell Obsession this.

I never said I was sane.
I share this story as I witnessed
Listen for Chrissake —

nôhkom rose high, filled the forest lodge.
Showed many pages of her face:
awâsis êkwa nôtokwêsiw
She arrives nightly, this bleeding sun
feather-mists over my breast,
scarred belly and seared thighs.
Stretches at dawn, shifts her wrinkles
to close one sun
(the other a wide-eyed heaven).
My *nôhkomis.*

Horse Liniment and the Boys

The old people wear that smell.
I think to kill Father-What-A-Waste.

I've gathered this from Mechanic,
this before *ospwâkan* left,
this before *wâpistikwân*, my father, lived.
Make of it what you will,
this story.

> *I am called* wiyipiyiniw, *filthy man, a bastard.*
> *Because of me mother will stay in hell. To all*
> *of you bunch of bitches* – pisikwâtisak, *mens*
> *are bastards.*
>
> *I was shipped to St. Judas. Spoke little English,*
> *hid my Cree. Cut my braids. I thought someone died.*
> *I wanted charcoal to paint my cheeks. Father-What-A-Waste*
> *became a hornet, unbuckled his belt. My breath ran those*
> *hallways. I fought. His neck was a cobra. Sister threw ice water, a*
> *scrub brush, lye soap. I burned. Forced cod-liver oil.*
> *I vomited and vomited. Licked the floor.*
> *Sacred old man buggered me. Bastards. How can I share this?*

wâpisikwân, my father, Mechanic.
they were never sorry.
ospwâkan on his knees
by the toilet.

White Island

Rolling Head took me for a stroll.
My boots and pants soaked
from last night's rain, slipped
on lichen, my foot wedged.
Rolling Head guided me to
a coyote's den, this
became my lair.

             There,
she said,
             you will pick your lover out of your skin.

For years I dug through that coyote's tunnel.
The water ship of childhood dreams
emerged as I struggled to surface.
When my head peered through
mother's hole,
a heat of bullets,
the rolling thunder of wheels
seared over me.
I slipped back into that muddy place.

I had not yet heard
about the battles my ancestors fought.
Yet
through my youth
I followed my Beloved's green eyes.
He carried my grandfather's stature,
leaned into the land
his ancestors bought for ten dollars in
1912.

But
Rolling Head swallowed my lover and me.
In her cavity
we made love,
sweating to tear our skins apart.

I have a white island
on my left hip
I share with my Beloved,
foreigner on my brown nakedness.
Though I've made love with my lover
I've never touched
his flesh.

In The Darkness of the Rolling Head

In the curved breast of the hills
Three Person and I, and the rest of the dreamers,
wide-eyed share a story or two.
We leave spaces.   Infinite spaces.

The succession works.

Three Person pulled the tarp,
tied herself into the buffalo robe and slept.
Before the first bird sang someone
grabbed her ankles.
She clawed the bodiless fingers. Broke free.
Clutched her chest, contorted, she grabbed a fist.
Sobs heaved. Mucus ran. In lucid moments,
she noticed teeny spiders skate on the globs.
Bunched grass. Rolling Head is mounds of earth,
standing wood, a cricket. Three Person
was with *pâhkahkos*, on the road to deliver
poultice to the sufferers. *pâhkahkos* jeered in her ear.
Problems were medicine.
When she got a flat tire. It was medicine.
When she didn't get a job. It was medicine.
When she got sunstroke. Medicine.
When the bingo passed her. Medicine.
Drank Buckley's. Polysporin wormed her cuts.
Antibiotics gave her trots. White man's medicine.

Maybe it was Onion Man, *aspin*
mâtahikan, perhaps her old lover Delicious
Fork. Maybe her heart-eating children. So
many curses. Over and over Rib Woman
played back her projector.

I, *ê-kweskit*, don't know if Three Person
walked through the dark.

Antelope Canyon, Arizona

A Navajo guide explained that the canyon will devour
People during unexpected flash floods. Flat sandstone bleeds
into ribbons of orange, yellow and red that twisted and swirled on this
desert rock. I saw no canyon where the guide stood. Uncomprehending
I saw my husband disappear into a slip within the earth. I followed,
Still not digesting that we had entered my mother's womb.
The walls contracted and we held our breath as we squeezed
Between the swollen desires, and walked the canals' long and windy gut.
Occasionally a sunbeam broke through the upper mouths
and we stood haloed inside a uterine cave.

I wonder what the eye of my husband's musical organ sees when
He enters my cave. A lodge of pulsing membrane, rivers of orange mud,
And walls of flames, this contraction of squeezing hallways birthing his
Juicy froth, the intoxication rushing as if a salmon's spawn swimming
toward their hibernation. My blossom a butterfly wing fluttering and
closing, grasping, gasping for this breath.

We followed the long valley of the canyon's trail and climb upward to
Spill against the ground. At this vaginal past lay open the large molars
Of the canyon's distant walk. In labored breath we walked in silence
Having been struck by the lightening of our birth.

Dedication to the Seventh Generation

ahâw,
ôta ka-wîhtamâtin aâcimisowin
I will share these stories
but I will not share
those from which I will never crawl.
It is best that way.
l forget to laugh sometimes,
though in these forty years
my life has been filled
with towering mornings,
northern lights.

Sit by the *kotawân* – the fire place.
Drink muskeg and mint tea.
Hold your soul
but do not weep.
Not for me, not for you.
Weep for those who haven't yet sung.
Weep for those who will never sing.

Burning in This Midnight Dream

I dream I wore a skin of X's across my chest
and down my torso. Granny prints of the midnight world.
Thick lenses moved inside my skull
magnifying but still I could not see.
The X awkwardly signed by my great grandmother
another burned ink onto my skin for Treaty Six,
X for the five dollar-a-year allotment,
X stitched for medicine, eye glasses, teeth,
and for school.
X for every sin, X for moments of grace.
The X's of a long paper chain wrapped this body.

The tattoos beckoned me not to surrender
to wear a grizzly cape
to dance until the sun's flames and moon beams
created passion inside my womb.
I was earth, burning in this midnight dream.

The Reserve Went Silent

The playground went silent.
A lone robin hopped in the expanse of the yard
where once children scraped their elbows and knees
drew lines in the dirt for hopscotch
or designated the imaginary rooms of a house
and lined the cupboards with mud pies.
The yard now empty, where once a lively
baseball field of excited runners
wore out trails between first base and third.
Where once the home base was a tattered
mound of scraped up dirt and scraggly grass.

I see this now.

I never saw the searing pain
on my mother's face, nor experienced
my father's eyes squeezed to dam his flood.
Their world went mute when the pied piper
played his organ through the reservation.
My parents never spoke
of the gash that tore through the families
and gutted the whole reserve.

Con Game

The children were meat
for the scavengers. Indian Affairs, the brick walls,
the Saints of many churches.
Filled with their disease, we ate the maggots
off their dead.
This cannibalism devoured our mother's hearth.

Yes, I followed this routine:
clapping hands and electric light,
on our knees to give the Christ
a difficult time, no time to rub the sleep
from our eyes. Each month I counted the stars
to see how often I'd gone to mass
my heart so wanting. March to breakfast,
to the scullery, hand-peel potatoes,
wash the many pots and pans
under the supervision of the kitchen nuns.
To the laundry room to starch and iron,
to the rectory to serve the higher saints
and finally to school to swallow Europe.

In those many seasons our winds
took a turn and entered winter.
When we were released
with no hair to braid,
no language to call our own
no parent to cradle us
those storms awoke.

His Name Was Boy

What to say about my brother
at Blue Quills he bent to tie my skates
his fingers
stiff from the icy wind.
In the dining room he crept
up to my table and
left a sucker.
At home he drew a jack-in-the beanstalk
hopscotch and challenged me to win.

Later he had me gallop
between his legs.
Tried to sell me to our cousin
behind the plank door.

He had learned well
from the residential school
priests, and other boys.

When we were going without food and water,
lamenting in the forest
the sugar chewed both his legs
ate his kidneys and took his breath.

This March when the wind
swirled snow across the road
obscured my vision
I gave his restless spirit
tobacco.

That night in sleep, here
by my bed,
he arrived with a thump
did his little dance
and left.

Sentinels

Awoken from the sleeping forest I listened
to the distant arrival of sound. I listened
from far away to this arrival
of souls.
Their moccasins shuffling to the thunderbird dance.
They arrived from the dark sky, a trail
of brilliant night dancers, the swish of skirts,
a man's thump. Yes, here. In my bedroom.
Three months now, on many nights they would steal
my slumber. Finally I asked
what was it they wanted. Only
their muteness answered.

I travelled to the red baked soil
where the midnight people
with long decorated earlobes wore beaded chokers
and wrapped red plaid shawls around their slenderness.
I travelled east among the relatives who ate guts
and heads of animals, beetles, scorpions,
sea-urchins, sold dehydrated snakes, bladders
and herbs. They clogged not only their streets,
but the air I inhaled.
l burned incense at their temples, honored their gods,
spoke to my Creator.
Not done with roaming
I watched Mount Etna spew over
our car, rounded the curves of skin-tight streets
roved the full-breasted hills of Sicily
never certain where the roads would go.

Months later when all was still
in the thick forest of dreams I woke to the joyous
drum-beat of the dancers, they arrived
faster than I remembered, here quickly.

When the last leaf fell, my ancient mother
told my sisters and I,
"*ninêstosin*. I am so tired."
Her journey a landscape of sugar-beet fields

chicken-scratches and kitchen terrors
on her deerskin face.
The last small wind blew slow and gentle,
carried her as she planted a smoking rose
on all our mouths.

misasiniy – large rock

I have a rock with four nodules
attached like two sets of Siamese twins.
They are the four heavens of my universe
the family of four I was born into
the four that we are
the four seasons, the four directions.
It holds me when I am buckling.

No number of prayer beads
strung through my fingers
could release me from this nether world.
All I need
is to hold this rock.

Still I wonder
how long this possession will last.

ospwâkan – the pipe

He sat between the women.
Told the story of how the ancient Elders
taught white men and their native brides
that their half-blood children had no right
to the Pipe, to the ceremonies.
How this teaching applied to this present day.
When these people, he prophesied,
took their last breath
they would remain as wandering ghosts
disturbing the present peace of their lost land.

When the women
spoke of their ancient grandmothers,
spoke of being outcasts
and how this applied to this present age,
they spoke of their love of their mixed-blood children,
the love they shared with their men.
The condemnation that walked from that man's tongue
cut their blood line and spilled it.
They arose and left him
with his bitterness and hate.
Returned to their families.

The Quandry

I have stripped my soul of the visions, the dreams
I received, given them all away. Still I continue
to wait each day, every night for more to come.
They dance softly, reluctant to reveal for fear
I'd give again what I've received.
But if I don't do this what will you know?
Your bitterness will gnaw, when
what was needed went to the grave
without having been spoken.
nôhkom and *nimosôm* left us without their voice,
without this story of *pimâtisiwin*, this culture
except the little that we saw.
Now I am a nothing person.
I cannot share what I don't know.
This endless search is meant to fill what I lost,
what is needed for this red road.
So I give these visions, share these dreams.
They have been my guides
in these many years of struggle.

Don't tell anyone of your visions, your dreams
they say, or they will leave you.
But my heart has no desire to remain tight-lipped
not because she needs validation
for receiving these messages,
not because she lacks humility.
She knows what it's like to crawl,
to beg to know
how to Sun Dance,
what offering she needed to make;
to know what to see in her Vision Quest,
what to expect. To know how to behave
at a Horse Dance, how to give at a Ghost Dance.
How to listen in a Shake Tent.
How to interpret the dreams,
these visions she received.
How can they teach, help.

Each day I am born again
to wander, to wonder, to listen,
to learn.

"it was a pure"

For you
"it was a pure"
longing burn like watching fire
creep on a piece of paper or a matchstick
fire blistering her finger tips. She recognized you
as while you walked through the woods,
sunlight against your dirty dark hair.
You've nestled into her shoulder
for the last forty years
lips pressed into her forehead.
If she could she would confess
all of her transgressions burden you
with sorrow but what was the point
to that? You can't live on that love alone,
you said one day as you counted
the last of your grandfather's coins
so you could have shelter for another
month and have a meal of macaroni.
She would tell your children
much later how you worked
as a carpenter building log cabins,
how an old girlfriend showed up
while breastfeeding your first born.
She would show them the diamond you
gave her for your fortieth anniversary.
For you, "it was a pure."

God of Nightmares

She thinks of the man who was eaten by his pancreas
how she moped through those biting days
how she stood like Romeo at the hospital window
wishing he was Raphael, she'd climb his hair
and tear it out of his skull
all this for setting her on fire.
But she thanks the god of nightmares
that it was only a few years
that she was imprisoned in the convent
of her books. Those questioning years he stole
the nights where her husband gazed
wondering to where she had disappeared.
She thanks the god of nightmares
that the acidic fire left blisters on pages
where her pen rose to meet the spirit
of answers her eyes searching
through the bibles of philosophy, psychology
sweat lodges, fasting and marriage contracts.
All those years she rode that fire's tail
whipping herself to frenzy for having fallen
into the gluttony of desire.

Afterword / *Sky Dancer Louise Bernice Halfe*

Sôhkêyihta. Have courage. Be brave. Be strong. Sôhkêyihta is a gentle, commanding word used to encourage people to stand strong while they face adversity. In order to move forward one must have the stamina, sometimes, to excise the oozing infection of a wound. I believe all that I have written has been about that excavation. Therefore, I encourage readers to stay grounded as they encounter their own shadows, or their own truths, in these stories. I walk. Meditate. Wrestle. I've pulled out my heart, wrung and strung it on the clothesline. These stories are a cumulative tear, a ceremonial gathering. That is why we sing, dance, and pray. Sôhkêyihta.

I am sitting quietly at my desk releasing the roar of the lawn mower. I've been cutting grass and, inhaling the scent of field and dust, thinking of the times I've been lost in a blizzard whiteout. In my desperation and need to hear nêhiyawêwin, the language of my soul and spirit, I start replying in Cree to the English speakers. When I was a little girl playing in the meadow before I left for residential school I spoke only nêhiyawêwin. I was not yet marked by the foreigners' spurious tongue. Yet in my broader social life I use English to communicate. When my recent grandson emerged from the womb I greeted him as kâ-nîkani, One Who Leads. It was as if the word too had emerged from the womb. I was startled by the force of its arrival. When my children were growing up I didn't strive enough to teach them Cree. I was too immersed in learning how to love and how to parent. When we returned to the prairies I embarked to embrace my nêhiyawêwin. The journey has had many twists and turns, but eventually I found myself fulfilling prophetic dreams. Though I am a Cree speaker it wasn't until I started to write that I examined the spirit of the language and found the ancient ones embedded within the sound and its speech. I have no secrets to disclose about writing in the Cree text. I have a need to preserve, to explore and help release the mysteries and musicality of my parental tongue.

Long before I understood writing, I wrote as a suicidal teenager, poems about lost hope, wandering the reserve looking for my skin, my kin. In my hopelessness, I wrote poems about my funeral and wept as I took pity upon myself. In my twenties, while living in a tent in Kootenay Plains alongside my parents, the prophetic dreams began. However I didn't understand them until I undertook ceremony, lifted up the pen and wrote. Then I remembered those dreams. My grandfather guiding my hand on the syllabics, lifting the Pipe on an earth altar, the cabin where I lost my dreams. On paper I realized the path where I would walk.

I grew up on the Saddle Lake Reserve in a log shack plastered with mud and straw. We were surrounded by woods, small meadows, and a couple of sloughs from where our water was hauled. In these woods I learned to walk quietly, for we were hunters and even a whisper was not allowed for fear we'd frighten away the night's supper. However, I found the forest spooky and frightening. There were times my mother, little sister, and I crisscrossed the woods seeking safety from the unpredictable nature of my father. Creeping is what we did between fear and apprehension.

In the mid-eighties my husband, our children, and I lived just outside the provincial forest in northern Saskatchewan. After my husband left for work and our children for school I'd grab pen and paper, and perhaps a book I had been reading, and head into the woods. At first my steps were tentative. I listened to the sounds that surrounded me. I'd stop, scribble in my journal whatever I heard or whatever caught my eye. In my previous life I wasn't much of a reader because I didn't grow up with books. But because I was spending so much time alone I consumed books like an emaciated coyote. Needless to say I had a lot of questions, which I learned to intuitively answer. Eventually I noticed that the writing was taking on its own quest and poetry poured from my fingers. Here I remembered my prophetic dreams and the affirmed message from the late Joe P. Cardinal: "You will write from the pages of the universe."

I've also had a fascination and love of the aurora borealis and its many shades of colours. Driving home from Alberta late one night the sky was lit up by the brilliant red, dancing skirts of these ancestors. Another night, different hues of green blended into the brush and prairie grass hovered over the landscape. Transformation, a celestial brush painted into the heavens where the grandparents walk and swirl. They are particularly active when they hear the heartbeat of the drum. When the Old Man presented my name Sky Dancer and explained its significance I knew without a doubt that all along I had been her. I've watched the scroll of my life unfold as he prophesied. This heavenly walk which I have been honoured to take I return to the reader.

I came across an advertisement in a Native journal, calling for Aboriginal women to submit their works for potential publication. I thought, "What have I got to lose?" and I mailed in some journal entries and a few poems. I received a very encouraging letter of acceptance from the anthology, *Writing the Circle: Native Women of Western Canada,* which was published in 1990. I also received an invitation to meet with the editors in Edmonton. I called upon Sylvia Vance, who kindly informed me that I had a "gift" and I should follow this calling. I was also taking satellite classes from the University of Saskatchewan, which is where I met Ron Marken, my English professor. He noticed my natural ability, though it was poorly formed, and encouraged me to continue the exploration. It was a thrill to have my work acknowledged and to be encouraged.

Memory is elusive at the best of times, and I can't recall how I learned about the Sagehill Writing Program, which offered a ten-day retreat with established writers. I applied and was accepted. There I met another mentor, Patrick Lane. It was through Sagehill that word got around to publishers about my developing manuscript, *Bear Bones & Feathers.* It was exciting to be among so many high-profile writers and to have my work seriously considered and eventually published by Coteau Books. Coteau Books continues to publish all my books. Ironically, I was informed by a senior poet that *Bear Bones & Feathers* may be the only good book I ever wrote. This same person also told me to embark on another project as soon as I could, because depression usually settles in after the long labour and birth of writing and publishing.

My biggest fear at that time was how my original family might perceive and receive the work. The stories spoke to some of their experiences, as the poems are not only of the self but are of the community fabric. Reaction was mixed. Some people were proud and encouraging. Others thought it had nothing but sexual content and went so far as to burn the book. Interestingly it was also censored in Norway House, Manitoba, where I had been initially invited to read at their college. That invitation was withdrawn. The content was clearly too controversial. I was pleased that the book raised their hackles and knew my work had hit home.

I wondered what I would write about next as I ruminated and fumbled with my thoughts. An Elder asked me what my next subject would be. Elders have an interesting way of encouraging the journey. I thought

I'd probably not write again. I laughed and said I wanted to rewrite history. Having spoken the thought aloud, I immediately pictured my four grandmothers, whose loves and lives I had limited knowledge of. So I quested, listened, and wrote. During the gestation of *Blue Marrow*, I had several more dreams that affirmed the project and I worked them into that epic poem. McClelland & Stewart approached me for the manuscript, but a series of editors struggled with the content. My new friend, Tim Lilburn, was the eventual editor. *Blue Marrow* was shortlisted for the Governor General's Award. The Indigenous Performance Initiatives (IPI) collective and Geraldine Manossa staged a collection of dance works inspired by *Blue Marrow*, called *Cipiyak Kanimihitotow*, at Trent University in 2009. My brother-in-law, who is a playwright, also developed a theatrical script, though that has yet to be produced. After *Blue Marrow* was released, I went back to my home reserve and had a ceremonial round-dance to honour my deceased grandmothers, who had guided me throughout the development of *Blue Marrow*. I believe in understanding and interpreting my dreams. It is important to pay attention to them as they hold the keys to laughter and problem-solving. They may also be prophetic. The dreams in essence are our guides.

When my grandsons were small I often reiterated the legend of the "Rolling Head" or cihcipistikwân âtayôhkêwin to them. I had learned it as a child. I was haunted by this story and in my aging questioned exactly how much Catholicism played into its evolution. I presented an analysis of the story at a Winnipeg writers' conference and gave it its first reading. Later, I embarked on its epic journey to become *The Crooked Good*, with my mother as the narrator of the story. Legends, such as cihcipistikwân âtayôhkêwin, were told in the winter when it was quiet and still and there was time out from harvesting and preparing for the winter. This was the time to sit around the fire and listen; children's imaginations could be ignited then. But it has been considered taboo, and I'm unsure why, to tell them at another season other than the winter months. Now work is distributed throughout the year and learning occurs in a more structured manner. Legends have to be told to be preserved. Our stories are being lost at an alarming rate due to language loss and community fragmentation. I believe it's important for the artists to preserve these stories in whatever genre the story finds its expression. Indigenous people are the keepers of these legends. Personally I don't want anthropologists to be the ones collecting and doing the preservation.

Burning in This Midnight Dream was conceived after I attended the Truth and Reconciliation gatherings in Saskatoon and Edmonton. I not only testified at one gathering but I also felt that the residential school experience had deeper ramifications than the stories we all shared. *Burning* had a voice that demanded to be heard. I had to trust that voice, even though doing so made me anxious and apprehensive. To ground and reassure myself I reread Matthew Fox, the author of *Original Blessings*. In his text he wrote:

> Facing the darkness, admitting the pain, allowing the pain to be pain, is never easy. This is why courage – big-heartedness – is the most essential virtue on the spiritual journey. But if we fail to let pain be pain, then pain will haunt us in nightmarish ways. We will become pain's victim instead of the healers we might become. And eventually pain's perpetrators.... Have insight into pain: enter it, befriend it ... there is no way to let go of pain without first embracing it and loving it – not as pain but as a sister and brother in our dialectical living of both pleasure and pain.... Pain is meant to give us energy. Pain is the most legitimate school for compassion.[1]

I hope we share in this process of spiritual enlightenment, intellectual observation, and emotional healing. Turn-Around Woman – ê-kwêskît in *The Crooked Good* – laments, "I am not a saint." I echo that thought. I do my best to be a good individual, but I have fallen short many times. These lessons I take to heart. I wonder where my soul had been at those particular moments and I seek self-forgiveness and forgiveness from those I may have harmed. These books are not only a journey of self but a journey of many whose voices have been muted by pain or community judgment. It is my hope that in this archeological excavation, this agitation of our bones, we can dust ourselves with lessons from the past and learn to live more fully. It is the lessons in our mistakes that teach us so much more about how rich life can be.

Note

1 Matthew Fox, *Original Blessing* (Bear & Company), 112–13.

Cree Glossary

Adapted from glossaries in *Bear Bones & Feathers*, *Blue Marrow*, and *The Crooked Good*

âcimo > tell stories, tell news
âcimostawinân > tell us stories
âcimowinisa > small stories
ahâw > All right, okay, that's it
asiskiy > 1. earth, 2. soil, 3. dirt, 4. clay, 5. mud
aspin > Gone-for-Good; used as a personal name
âstam > come, come here
âstamik pê-kîwêk > come (pl), come home (pl)
âtayôhkanak > spirit beings; spiritual entities; ancient legend spirits
câcaâmosikan > sneezing root
cahkipêhikana > syllabics
câpan > Great Grandmother or Great Grandfather; it is not gender specific
cihcipistikwân > Rolling Head
ê-kî-âhtaskêyan > s/he puts her/his land elsewhere
êkwa > and
iskwêw > woman
iskwêwak > women
Iyiniwak > People
kayâs êsa > ancient times; a long, long time ago
kayâs-âcimowin > ancient story
kisêwâtisiwin > kindness
kisêyiniwak > the very Elderly Men; they are held in high esteem
kîsik >1. sky, 2. the Heavens
kiskisiw > she remembers
kitânisak > your daughters
mâmaw-ôhtâwîmâw > Creator of All, Giver of Life
mâmitonêyihtêstamâsowin > to deliberate, to weigh thought

manawânis > a town; a place where one collects extra goods, i.e., food/cloth-
ing, tools; this word has other implications.
mâtahikan > a tool used for fleshing/scraping fur off of an animal skin
matotisân > the Sweatlodge; the lodge where All Relations bear witness of
tears and healing
môniyaw-kisêyiniw > old white man
nâpêsisak > boys
nîci > fellow, my friend
nikosisak > my sons
nimosôm > my grandfather
nipêpîmak > my babies
Nôhkom > my Grandmother
nôhkom âtayôhkan > Grandmother Keeper of the Sacred Legends
nôsisim > my grandchild
nôtokwêsiw > an old woman
nôtokwêsiw > old woman
nôtokwêsiwak > the very Elderly Women; they are held in high esteem
okâwîmâwaskiy > 1. Mother Earth, 2. Beyond the Horizon Earth Mother,
3. the Infinite Earth Mother
omikiya > scabs
ospwâkan > 1. pipe (for smoking); 2. used as a personal name, Pipe
Pâhkahkos > 1. Bony Spectre, Hunger spirit, spirit being; flying skeleton
pahkisimotâhk > 1. west, in the west, towards the sunset; 2. where the sun
falls, a falling away
pawâkan > 1. Dream Spirit, 2. Guardian of Dreams and Visions
pimâtisi > live
pimâtisiwin > life
pisikwâtisak > those who are bold with the opposite sex or commit adultery;
2. loose sexually
piyêsiwak > the Thunders
sâkâstêw > sunrise
sâkihitowin > love
sôhkêyimo > persevere, be brave
tawahikan > 1. the land/horizon of abundant beauty and life, 2. to clear a spot,
make a space, make room for
wâpan > 1. It is dawn, morning; 2. used as a personal name, Morning or Dawn
wâpâsôs > Early Riser
wâpistikwân > 1. white hair; 2. used as a personal name, White Hair
wâsatinaw > bright hill
wîhkês > rat root, a bitter medicinal root
wîhtam > he/she tells it

wîhtikow > cannibal, giant man-eating monster; 2. cannibalistic creature; not spoken about because of its intense power – especially during winter – or else famine will strike.

wîhtikow sâkahikan > Cannibal Lake; a fictitious name, a fabricated location

Wîsahkecâhk > Cree trickster

wiyin > fat

wiyipiyiniw > Filthy Man; used as a personal name in this story

yôtin > wind, it is windy

Acknowledgements

With thanks to Brian Henderson, Neil Besner, Siobhan McMenemy, and Lisa Quinn from Wilfrid Laurier University Press. Thanks also to John Agnew and Coteau Books for making these poems available for this collection.

* * *

I would like to thank Wilfrid Laurier University Press for taking on this project and David Gaertner for carrying it through. In particular, I'd like to extend appreciation to the readership, for the teachers/professors using my poetics and bringing it to the larger audience. Truly my heart is full. I'd like to acknowledge my husband, children, and grandchildren, and my home community, who went into ceremony with me to honour this gift of writing and story sharing. To each and every one of the editors as well as various friends who read the various manuscripts in their entirety, nanâskom.

—Louise

* * *

I would like to thank Sophie McCall and Deanna Reder for reading drafts of the Introduction and for their wise and generative feedback. Thank you to Sarah Hunt and Daniel Justice for their insight and guidance on this project. Thank you also to Carleigh Baker and the UBC Indigenous Lit Reading Group for reading these poems out loud with me and sharing their thoughts and ideas. Thanks to Dallas Hunt for his help with Cree syllabics. Thanks especially to Warren Cariou for his mentorship and support of this book. Most of all, thanks to Louise Halfe for these poems and for the kindness and inspiration you gift in all of your work.

—David

* * *

Contents and Sources

"Crying for Voice," "der poop," and "Body Politics," are from *Bear Bones & Feathers* (Coteau Books, 1994). "The Residential School Bus," "Thieves," and "Returning" were originally published in *Residential Schools: The Stolen Years* (Linda Jaine, ed., University of Saskatchewan Extension Press, 1993) and were republished in *Bear Bones & Feathers* with minor revisions. "pâhkahkos," "Nôhkom, Medicine Bear," and "Valentine Dialogue" were originally published in *Writing the Circle: Native Women of Western Canada* (Jeanne Perrault and Sylvia Vance, eds., NeWest Press, 1990) and republished in *Bear Bones & Feathers* with minor revisions. Excerpts from *Blue Marrow* are from the 2004 Coteau Books edition. *Blue Marrow* was originally published by McClelland & Stewart in 1998. The Coteau version was revised by Halfe and includes additional text and a Cree-to-English dictionary. Poems may vary slightly across editions. "Listen: To the Story," "ê-kwêskît – Turn-Around Woman," "The Tracker," "Everyday Is a Story," "Excavating," "Horse Liniment and the Boys," "White Island," and "In the Darkness of the Rolling Head" are from *The Crooked Good* (Coteau Books, 2009). "Antelope Canyon" was first published in *ARC Poetry Review*. "Dedication to the Seventh Generation," "Burning in This Midnight Dream," "The Reserve Went Silent," "Con Game," "His Name Was Boy," "Sentinels," "*misasiniy* – large rock," "*ospwâkan* – the pipe," and "The Quandry" are from *Burning in This Midnight Dream* (Coteau, 2016). "it was a pure" and "God of nightmares" were first published in *The Malahat Review*.

lps Books in the Laurier Poetry Series
Published by Wilfrid Laurier University Press

Fred Wah   *The False Laws of Narrative: The Poetry of Fred Wah*, edited by Louis Cabri, with an afterword by Fred Wah • 2009 • xxiv + 78 pp. • ISBN 978-1-555458-046-0

Tom Wayman   *The Order in Which We Do Things: The Poetry of Tom Wayman*, edited by Owen Percy, with an afterword by Tom Wayman • 2014 • xx + 92 pp. • ISBN 978-1-555458-995-1

Jan Zwicky   *Chamber Music: The Poetry of Jan Zwicky*, edited Darren Bifford and Warren Heiti, with a conversation with Jan Zwicky • 2014 • xx + 82 pp. • ISBN 978-1-77112-091-3